A STUDY OF *THUMOS*
IN EARLY GREEK EPIC

MNEMOSYNE
BIBLIOTHECA CLASSICA BATAVA

COLLEGERUNT

A. D. LEEMAN · H.W. PLEKET · C. J. RUIJGH

BIBLIOTHECAE FASCICULOS EDENDOS CURAVIT

C. J. RUIJGH, KLASSIEK SEMINARIUM, OUDE TURFMARKT 129, AMSTERDAM

SUPPLEMENTUM CENTESIMUM DECIMUM QUARTUM

CAROLINE P. CASWELL

**A STUDY OF *THUMOS*
IN EARLY GREEK EPIC**

A STUDY OF *THUMOS* IN EARLY GREEK EPIC

BY

CAROLINE P. CASWELL

E.J. BRILL
LEIDEN · NEW YORK · KØBENHAVN · KÖLN
1990

ISSN 0169-8958
ISBN 90 04 09260 9

© *Copyright 1990 by E. J. Brill, Leiden, The Netherlands*

All rights reserved. No part of this book may be reproduced or translated in any form, by print, photoprint, microfilm, microfiche or any other means without written permission from the publisher

PRINTED IN THE NETHERLANDS

To Jonathan, Christian and Adam.

CONTENTS

Acknowledgements IX
I. θυμός: A Statement of the Problem 1
II. A Summary of Previous Studies of θυμός 5
III. An Analysis of the Usage of θυμός in Early Greek Epic 11
IV. θυμός Examined Further: Connections with the Winds 51
Appendix 65
Bibliography 79
Index 81

ACKNOWLEDGEMENTS

Heartfelt thanks to all those who encouraged me to persist in this effort and gave me much good advice. In particular, I would like to thank Gregory Nagy, who never flinched at the audacity of my undertaking, and Carl Ruck, who was unfailingly kind and supportive. My thanks go also to Emily Hanawalt for her support and to Charles Beye for his trenchant criticism and support.

This work is, I hope, a small contribution to a field of enormous questions, many of them no doubt unanswerable. Any errors of execution or reasoning are my responsibility alone.

CHAPTER ONE

ΘΥΜΟΣ: A STATEMENT OF THE PROBLEM

The most-used psychological term in Homeric diction has received little attention since Joachim Böhme published his work *Die Seele und das Ich im Homerischen Epos* in 1929. Both he and R. B. Onians in his *Origins of European Thought* undertook to discuss all the terms relating to early Greek psychology and physiology, Böhme concentrating on the psychology and Onians blending the two. These ambitious enterprises, hampered somewhat by the wish to discover a logical system for the Homeric terminology of inner experience, allowed for too little attention to be given to variations in the use of θυμός. Therefore, although these works remain most valuable,[1] the conclusions are insufficient for a clearer understanding of the semantic range of θυμός.

The problem is well-known. Generations of classicists and readers of Homer both in the original and in translation have been making do with approximations in meaning which range from "soul" to "anger", but it is clear that these words do not adequately express what was intended by the Greek. And yet the uses of θυμός are so varied, covering almost every important aspect of inner human experience, that it seems possible only to translate each occurrence as is fitting to that passage without attempting consistency. Under these circumstances, there is definitely a need for a thorough investigation of the semantic range of θυμός. In his book *Nature and Culture in the Iliad*, James M. Redfield has identified θυμός with the breath and has added a challenge thereto:

> θυμός is the seat of the whole practical consciousness, from instant rage and pain to planning and deliberation on the basis of lessons laboriously learned. This practical intelligence, in Homer, is presented as a single phenomenon and at the same time with extraordinarily subtle internal differentiation; a careful taxonomy of the whole range of verbal ideas associated with θυμός would reveal the complexity of the implicit empirical analysis and would illuminate much in the poems.[2]

In keeping with this keen estimation of the problem, I hope in the course of my "careful taxonomy" to arrive not so much at a translation as at a clearer, more detailed understanding of the associations of θυμός in its contexts. For two not entirely unconnected reasons, I do not wish to focus

---

[1] Böhme's work was indispensable to this study — thorough, painstaking, and often a necessary support for checking the contexts of passages.

[2] Redfield, 1975, 174.

on the problem of translation. First of all, the range of usage is so extensive and the apparent synonyms so numerous that it is of prime importance to understand better the semantic associations of θυμός itself. Second, in the course of making this analysis, I have not found a word or phrase which could serve as an adequate universal equivalent. That is not to say categorically that there is none; as mentioned above, there are existing approximations of meaning. But the complexity of the problem of translation could perhaps better be dealt with in a separate study. In order to carry out the proposed analysis of θυμός in early Greek epic, I examined every relevant passage in Homer, Hesiod and the Homeric Hymns. It became apparent during this stage of my research that the passages from the *Iliad* are of greater interest because they include a greater variety of expressions. Passages from the *Odyssey*, Hesiod and the Homeric Hymns tend to greater predictability or repetition and therefore offer less insight into the visualization of the inner processes with which this work is concerned. Therefore, in general, the *Iliad* is quoted more often; but all texts concerned have an absolutely vital bearing on the conclusions.

The need for thoroughness and consistency suggested an adaptation of Böhme's system[3] for the categorization of passages according to the type of context in which θυμός occurs; but since I wished to adhere as closely as possible to the actual categories of function, it seemed necessary to add two additional ones. The categories are as follows: 1) loss of consciousness/ death[4] 2) the cognitive or intellectual function, 3) the emotional function, 4) the deliberative function, and 5) the function of motivation. It will be seen that within categories 1), 4) and 5) θυμός occurs in combination with certain other words, and that these combinations are required by Homeric diction in order to describe adequately the subtle nuances of inner experience.

Since the contexts of usage have been established for θυμός, it is possible to proceed with a systematic review of each set of associations and functional synonyms. In the first context, that of loss of consciousness/ death, it is apparent that, although θυμός/μένος/ψυχή are functional synonyms at the moment of loss of consciousness, θυμός and ψυχή diverge depending on whether revival or death occurs subsequently: θυμός is the element which returns to the body upon revival; ψυχή, on the other hand, is that which survives death; and μένος[5] apparently can be connected only with a living

---

[3] Böhme discovered rightly that there was a relationship between the physical and the psychological in the case of θυμός. But he studied the word more as it related to his own view of psychology and inner experience, not to the view of epic diction. Hence he discussed it in the contexts of cognition (a problem), emotion, and death/loss of consciousness only.

[4] Nagy, 1980.

[5] The question of μένος is complex and not central to the approach I have taken here,

body, like θυμός. Clearly there is a connection in this context between θυμός and the breath, as we will see later from specific associations. For the second or cognitive context, the evidence is less abundant. The use of θυμός as an element in the intellectual function, however, is significant. It occurs with a number of verbs, for example οἶδα, γιγνώσκω, φρονέω, νοέω and φράζω; and it seems to stand in a specific relationship to φρήν/φρένες/ νόος. There emerges a new concept, that of containment: in order for a person to think properly, his θυμός needs to be contained within the φρήν/ φρένες. Hence, although usually θυμός occurs as an element in emotional experience, it can also be active during cognition, particularly when it is properly located. Containment of θυμός, when it exists, changes considerably the way in which his θυμός affects the individual. Within the third, or emotional, context, θυμός occurs most often. It is used with the functional synonyms φρήν/φρένες/ἦτορ/κραδίη but is far more frequent there as the element which experiences emotion. Again, there is the suggestion of a specific relationship to the φρήν/φρένες. A small number of passages in which θυμός alone is used, for example with φιλέω and δαμάζω, also express a spatial relationship specific to the emotion experienced. In the context of deliberation, θυμός/φρήν/φρένες/ἦτορ function as synonyms. This context is unusual because θυμός and φρήν/φρένες are found very often in parallel construction, implying complete equality between the two.

In the context of deliberation, θυμός/φρήν/φρένες/ἦτορ function as synonyms. This context is unusual because θυμός and φρήν/φρένες are found very often in parallel construction, implying complete equality between the two.

In the fifth context, that of motivation, θυμός/μένος/κραδίη function as synonyms. The decided preference is for θυμός and μένος in parallel construction with the verb ὀτρύνω. The φρήν/φρένες, which occur with θυμός as the container in the context of cognition, are most important in understanding the connotations of this context. Also significant is the fact that θυμός occurs alone with the verbs ὀρίνω, ἐπισσεύω, κέλομαι, ἐφορμάω, and ἐποτρύνω.

Finally, we find that θυμός has associations in more than one context with words relating to the actions of winds and storms. It occurs in several striking weather similes which are used to describe the nature of inner turmoil in men.

Therefore, it will become clear that there is an underlying system to the usage of θυμός in Homeric diction. I have already mentioned the concept of containment which is inherent in certain occurrences of θυμός with φρήν/

---

although its relationship to θυμός would be well worth further study. It is used on both the animal/human and the cosmic levels. See Nagy 1980 for an extensive treatment.

φρένες; lack of containment also occurs and is emphasized not only by the absence of φρήν/φρένες in some cases but by the connotations of the verbs with which it is used. This concept leads ultimately to the visualization of θυμός as an inner wind, a visualization which is reinforced by its own etymology.⁶ When the use of θυμός is re-examined with the help of this new information, its breadth of application will become understandable. It will become clear that at the period during which the Homeric epics were being formed, θυμός was at the foundation of every internal experience or manifestation.⁷ Θυμός as found in Homeric diction is both fundamental and specific. When the passages are carefully examined, it will be seen that θυμός cannot be considered entirely interchangeable with its functional synonyms in every context; and we will understand a little better why that is.

---

⁶ Böhme, 1929, 22–23.
⁷ Onians, 1954, 44–65; Böhme, 1929, 74–83.

CHAPTER TWO

A SUMMARY OF PREVIOUS STUDIES OF ΘΥΜΟΣ

The semantics of θυμός has received sporadic attention over the past century, having been somewhat slighted in favor of efforts in relation to ψυχή. Erwin Rohde discussed at length the problem of the Homeric concepts of death and the soul in his monumental work *Psyche*, dealing by the way as it were with the problem of θυμός. Under the influence of Spencer, he accepted the idea that the Greeks shared "a mode of thought that lies so close to the mind of primitive mankind,"[1] in other words the concept of a shadowy double without φρένες which is active only when the man himself is asleep, unconscious, or dead. Since Homeric evidence for the activity of the ψυχή during dreams does not exist, Rohde made use of Pindar fragment 131b[2] to complete his case. In straining to raise his view of Homer beyond the "primitive", he concluded that ψυχή at this early period meant virtually "life", thus protecting early Greek epic from the possible accusation of fostering belief in a double which survives death and can therefore have an effect upon the world of the living. He saw φρήν/φρένες, θυμός, ἦτορ, κῆρ, and κραδίη as terms for inner functions which were still named after organs of the body and notes that "the mythology of the 'inner man' was breaking down altogether."[3] The bulk of the attention given to θυμός by Rohde is to be found in his footnote 58 to Chapter I, where he outlines briefly and accurately its province: that it did not survive death, that it was the seat of the emotions, and of thinking, i.e. that it was a faculty of the living body.

Joachim Böhme undertook an extensive and careful study of all Homeric psychological vocabulary in his work *Die Seele und das Ich im Homerischen Epos*. His work was a response to the earlier studies of Otto and Bickel, who had taken issue with Rohde's interpretation of ψυχή as a weaker double of the person. Böhme was not satisfied with the conclusions to which Otto and Bickel had come, that on the one hand ψυχή represented a "Totengeist" and that on the other hand it was also the "body-soul". It was clear to him that there was a need to come to a more exact understanding of just how ψυχή, θυμός, φρήν/φρένες, ἦτορ, κραδίη, μένος, and other terms functioned and related to each other and to the individual. Did Homeric poetry, in fact, know of the concept "life-soul"?

---

[1] Rohde, 6.
[2] ed. Snell, frg. 131b.
[3] Rohde, 30.

Böhme recognized that one of the difficulties of trying to define the inner functions lay in the merging of the physical and the psychological. In a sense he treated this problem with more respect than did Rohde, perhaps also because the extent of his undertaking forced him to examine a number of concepts in detail. But inevitably he was influenced by the thinking of his time and assumed that the "primitiveness" of the Greeks eliminated automatically any complex understanding, for example, of the organs of the body.[4] Like Rohde, he made a connection between ψυχή and ψύχω, "to blow or breathe", and hence to the meaning "life-soul" from "life-breath". He believed that the φρένες were the chief organ of the ego, since their function seems to be primarily intellectual.[5] He noted that θυμός functions mainly as an emotional faculty[6] but had difficulty in dealing with exceptional cases. Unlike Arbman, he did not attempt to see in θυμός a unified concept of "body-soul" but rather one of several life potencies. Ultimately he did not find in Homer the concept of the unified individual.

Böhme was also motivated by the aim of finding suitable translations for the various psychological terms of Homeric diction. It is out of this impulse that other difficulties arose for him in dealing more objectively with the evidence, for at times he tried to force his findings into a contemporary framework. Despite these criticisms of his attempts at conclusions, his work is thorough and useful and continues to be an excellent starting point for anyone interested in this subject.

Bruno Snell's book *The Discovery of the Mind* has been the departure for much work done more recently on the subject of Homeric psychology. He too saw the early Greeks as "primitive" thinkers, an attitude which is questionable. He tried to show logically that Homer's view of the individual is not unified and made a comparison between what he supposed to be the progression from archaic Greek thinking in this respect up to present-day views of the individual and the development in a child's view of the individual to the view of the adult. His use of the Greek language to support his hypothesis, and particularly his use of the fact that epic diction favors words for discrete parts of the body over words for the whole, gave his argument the appearance of having a solid linguistic base. But a recent article by Robert Renehan[7] has effectively challenged Snell's view of archaic Greek psychology by proving that the premises on which he based his arguments were unsound, and that the Homeric corpus cannot be considered sufficiently extensive to support Snell's *argumentum ex silentio*.

---

[4] Böhme, 8–9.
[5] *Ibid.*, 50.
[6] *Ibid.*, 60.
[7] Renehan 1979, 269–282.

Previous studies on Homeric psychology, and the present one, face the same dilemma: the search for a unified concept of either body or soul is frustrated repeatedly by a vocabulary which reflects no abstraction but rather a lively interest in detail.

In his book *The Origins of European Thought*, R. B. Onians dealt at length with many problems in both Greek and Latin of the understanding of physiological and psychological terms. He made extensive use of comparative evidence and approached the problem with considerably more open-mindedness than Snell. Nevertheless, the enormous range of his investigations made lengthy, detailed study of each word out of the question. His conclusions, though more definitive than Böhme's, are nevertheless not entirely convincing because of this brevity of treatment. However, it is important to mention them here since they have had influence on the conclusions of this paper. Onians not only made the connection between Latin *fumus* and Greek θυμός but justified it etymologically via Slavic cognates which developed the meanings "breath" and "spirit" by way of "smoke" and "vapor". He connected the meaning "breath" for θυμός with the concept of containment within the φρένες, which he defined as the lungs.[8] In addition, he entertained the possibility that θυμός could have referred to the vapor rising from warm blood. He was familiar with the concept of *praṇa* in the Upanishads:[9] "Our incredulity, if not our wonder, may be diminished when we realize that the ancient Hindoos had similar beliefs. According to the Upanishads, speech, sight, hearing, and mind were known as breaths (*praṇa*). 'Verily, they do not call them 'speeches' nor 'eyes' nor 'minds.' They call them 'Breaths,' for the vital breath is all these; ......'" Onians' definition of the φρένες as the lungs is still considered a possibility; and his suggestion that θυμός might refer to a concept similar to that of *praṇa* in Hindu thought is intriguing, if beyond the province of the present consideration.

In his study *Frühgriechischer Totenglaube: Untersuchungen zum Totenglaube der mykenischen und homerischen Zeit*, Albrecht Schnaufer makes use of both archaeological and literary evidence in his effort to discover the true nature of early Greek belief in the soul. Unfortunately his findings on

---

[8] Onians, 44. See Ireland and Steel 187–188 for a criticism of Onians' conclusions here and elsewhere. Note that at 193–194, they discuss the relationship of φρένες to the πραπίδες. In this connection, I quote Vernant, v. 1, 95:
  Comme M. Louis Gernet l'a fait observer, Empédocle se sert, pour désigner l'«ésprit», du vieux terme de πραπίδες, un de ces mots qui désignent à la fois, sans les distinguer nettement, un organe du corps et une activité «psychique;» πραπίδες, c'est proprement le diaphragme, dont la «tension» règle ou même arrête la respiration. On connaît, de reste, les liens qui unissent, dans la pensée grecque archaïque, l'âme et le souffle respiratoire.

[9] Onians, 75.

ψυχή have been questioned, since funerary practices do not necessarily indicate actual religious belief.[10] He defines θυμός as energy, not as consciousness,[11] giving as his reason that Homeric man was too primitive to be capable of self-consciousness, or conscious of the whole.

The article by Ireland and Steel[12] is a useful restatement of the problem, concentrating on the physical aspect. Conclusions, however, are not forthcoming: the authors stated that it was impossible to discover physiological exactitude in poetic material. Nagy's article "Patroklos,"[13] concentrating mainly on the problem of μένος ἠΰ, pinpoints some of the divergences between μένος, ψυχή and θυμός, which function as synonyms only at the moment of loss of consciousness/death, thus providing both a method and a point of departure for the present study. And in his article "The Causation of Death in the *Iliad*,"[14] Garland examines passages in which θυμός and ψυχή are the causes of death: the departure of either one or both result in death, but only θυμός seems to play a biological role.

Jan Bremmer's book *The Early Greek Concept of the Soul* is the most extensive recent work on ψυχή. He has found that the characteristics of ψυχή fit Arbman's definition of the "free-soul," and that ψυχή became the soul of the dead. In relation to ψυχή, then, θυμός, μένος and νόος correspond to the body-souls, as opposed to the free-soul of the living.[15] Douglas Frame's book *The Myth of Return in Early Greek Epic*,[16] which concentrates on the elucidation of the etymological and semantic relationship between νέομαι and νόος, provides ample proof that the company words keep, so to speak, can enhance significantly our understanding of Homeric vocabulary. The series of articles by Shirley Darcus on the φρήν/φρένες, νόος, ψυχή and so on from early Greek epic on up to the Presocratics provides a solid basis of information about how these words are used and what characteristics they display. Three recent articles by André Cheyns discuss the grammatical uses and contexts of: 1) θυμός, 2) φρήν/φρένες and 3) ἦτορ, κῆρ and κραδίη. The first two are more directly related to the topic of this paper. As in the articles by Darcus, there are a number of useful observations; and the conclusions drawn by Cheyns in his article on θυμός are close to the conclusions of this investigation. His article on the φρένες establishes the physical identification of the organ(s) as the lungs or the pericardium. Other books and articles mentioned in the notes and the

---

[10] Sourvinou-Inwood, 1972, 220–222.
[11] Schnaufer, 197.
[12] Ireland and Steel 1975, 183–195.
[13] Nagy 1980, 161–195.
[14] Garland 1981, particularly Table 2, 47.
[15] Bremmer, 54–58.
[16] Frame 1978.

bibliography deal with peripheral topics which are, however, essential to the points to be made in this study.

This rather abbreviated summary of previous work on θυμός (and necessarily, other psychological terms) is intended primarily as an explanation for the approach to be used in this study. The tool of synchronic formulaic analysis allows for the examination of each passage on its own terms, thus making less likely the drawing of conclusions about the material at hand from factors which are not strictly relevant. In this way, Homeric diction can be allowed to speak for itself. In order to facilitate the process, each occurrence of θυμός has been categorized in a manner already established by Böhme, except that epic diction itself suggested the addition of two smaller but significant groupings which could less easily be fitted into the existing classification. It is hoped that this categorization will be seen for what it is, merely a means to an end, and not as the harbinger of future conclusions.

This caution is based on a conviction which has its roots in the reading of early Greek epic, where love of detail generates poetic life and beauty and is an integral part of the diction; there is no place here for abstraction. Hence the concern of this study has been not with its absence but with a deeper understanding of the language as it is found, and of course particularly with a deeper understanding of θυμός. To the same end, translation of terms under investigation has been avoided throughout, as has the temptation to look upon Homeric thought as a precursor to our own. This is not to state categorically that there is no connection between the two, but that such questions do not come within the scope of this work. The forthcoming conclusions may enable us to judge whether this approach has been effective.

CHAPTER THREE

AN ANALYSIS OF THE USAGE OF ΘΥΜΟΣ IN EARLY GREEK EPIC

§1. Method: The search for a satisfactory definition of θυμός is attested by the entry in LSJ⁹, which presents a dizzying array of possibilities: *soul, spirit, as the principle of life, feeling and thought, esp. of strong feeling and passion* (rightly derived from θύω (B) by Pl. *Cra.* 419e. ἀπὸ τῆς θύσεως καὶ ζέσεως τῆς ψυχῆς).[1] The extent of its usage has remained a problem for classicists despite the publication of a number of studies. As mentioned in the previous chapter, Böhme and Onians made valuable discoveries; both were hampered not only by the scope of their task but by the fact that they attempted to fit the material either into a framework suggested by the possible logical progression of ideas from archaic Greek times to our own, or by recent anthropological findings. These attempts resulted in some distortions of the evidence, so valuable in its own right. The use of synchronic formulaic analysis guards against the temptation to pass qualitative judgments on the findings, since it allows only for the examination of the word in context. Moreover, although synonyms and associations of θυμός must naturally be discussed, the scope of this work is limited to a study of θυμός alone, in the belief that the results will thus be more informative.

§2. Categories: Each context in which θυμός occurs will be examined separately. As mentioned in the introduction, they are as follows: 1) loss of consciousness/death,[2] 2) cognition or the function of the intellect, 3) the function of emotion, 4) the function of deliberation, and 5) the function of motivation. It was mentioned in the introduction that the last two categories have been added to the system of classification used by Böhme. Strictly speaking, the fourth category can be seen as a combination of 2) and 3), and the fifth as a subcategory of the emotional context. However, Homeric diction itself makes definite distinctions in the way deliberation and motivation are described in terms of θυμός. It seems, therefore, more in keeping with the spirit of this investigation to adhere to the organization suggested by the evidence.

There are so many occurrences of θυμός in the Homeric corpus that not every passage can be discussed here. Robert Garland's article "The Causation of Death in the *Iliad*: A Theological and Biological Investigation"

---

[1] LSJ (9), 810.
[2] Nagy 1980, 162 ff.

surveys all occurrences of death and summarizes usage in tables. In each context, I will select certain passages for discussion; and the Appendix will afford the reader an overview of usage by grouping passages according to context and subcontext.

§3. Syncope: In the first context, that of loss of consciousness/death, θυμός functions as a synonym of μένος/ψυχή at the moment of loss of consciousness or death.[3] At V 696, Sarpedon falls into a swoon:

τὸν δὲ λίπε ψυχή, κατὰ δ' ὀφθαλμῶν κέχυτ' ἀχλύς·

And his ψυχή left him, and darkness poured down over his eyes.

At XXII 466–467, Andromakhe swoons and her ψυχή wafts from her like smoke:[4]

τὴν δὲ κατ' ὀφθαλμῶν ἐρεβεννὴ νὺξ ἐκάλυψεν,
ἤριπε δ' ἐξοπίσω, ἀπὸ δὲ ψυχὴν ἐκάπυσσε.

At V 698, Boreas returns to Sarpedon his κεκαφηότα θυμόν.[5] This passage is the only example in the *Iliad* where θυμός is the element lost in a swoon, and implicitly at that, by the use of the participle κεκαφηότα.[6] In general, then, ψυχή departs at syncope and the θυμός returns; μένος is not used at all. There are, therefore, no examples of complete semantic convergence between θυμός, ψυχή and μένος in this subcontext.

§4. Death: To continue by examining the behavior of θυμός in the subcontext of death, we see that at the moment of death it converges semantically with ψυχή, μένος, αἰών, and ἦτορ. In addition to cases which could be described as metaphorical,[7] there are a number of literal expressions. The αἰών leaves,[8] the ἦτορ is stripped away, the knees or limbs are loosed, and so on. The ψυχή can leave in a variety of ways, by going down to Hades at VII 330 and XVI 625, by crossing the barrier of the teeth at IX 408–409, by coming out of the fatal wound at XIV 518–519 and XVI 505, by flying from

---

[3] *Ibid.*, 183.

[4] In both cases θυμός returns, a fact which will be discussed later. Also, see Nagy 1980, 164.

[5] Chantraine 528 hesitates to connect κεκαφηότα with καπύειν because of the unexplained aspirate. Nagy 1983, 208–209, notes the importance of this passage in light of the eventual immortalization of Sarpedon.

[6] See Garland 1981, Table 6.

[7] *Ibid.* 47 ff.

[8] Solmsen 1979, in discussing the meaning of σύμφυτος αἰών, Aischylos' *Agamemnon* 105 f., opts for the meaning "marrow." Nagy 1981, 115, however, presents a view more in keeping with its occurence in the context of death: "The Greek adverb αἰεί corresponding to the noun αἰών is forever' in the original sense of a perpetual starting-over (e.g. 152), an eternal return." In considering the whole text, ἔτι γὰρ θεόθεν καταπνείει/πειθὼ μολπᾶν ἀλκὰν σύμφυτος αἰών, it seems possible to read the passage with both meanings in mind. They are not, if Nagy is right, mutually exclusive ideas.

the limbs at XVI 856 and XXII 362, etc.[9] In three cases in the *Iliad*, both ψυχή and μένος are loosed, the lines and the contexts being identical.[10] At XI 334 θυμός and ψυχή are removed.[11] At VIII 358, death is described as the falling away of μένος and θυμός.[12] Μένος alone departs only twice, at XVI 332 and XVII 298. The commonest element whose absence determines death is θυμός. Generally it departs in the same manner as its functional synonyms; and along with μένος, it ceases to exist as an entity once the process of death has been completed.

§5. Revival after syncope: It has been seen that at V. 696–698, ψυχή departs and θυμός returns:

τὸν δὲ λίπε ψυχή, κατὰ δ' ὀφθαλμῶν κέχυτ' ἀχλύς·
αὖτις δ' ἀμπνύνθη, περὶ δὲ πνοιὴ Βορέαο
ζώγρει ἐπιπνείουσα κακῶς κεκαφηότα θυμόν.[13]

His ψυχή left him, and darkness poured down over his eyes; but again he breathed, and the breath of the North Wind breathing upon him revived the θυμός which had grievously wafted away.[14]

The same is true at XXII 466–467 and 475:

τὴν δὲ κατ' ὀφθαλμῶν ἐρεβεννὴ νὺξ ἐκάλυψεν,
ἤριπε δ' ἐξοπίσω, ἀπὸ δὲ ψυχὴν ἐκάπυσσε.
....
ἡ δ' ἐπεὶ οὖν ἄμπνυτο καὶ ἐς φρένα θυμὸς ἀγέρθη,.....[13]

Dark night covered her eyes, and she fell back, and her ψυχή wafted off......
But when she breathed again and her θυμός was gathering back into her φρήν
.....

And at XV 240, Hektor is revived from a weakened state, not actual loss

---

[9] See Garland 1981, Table 7. Note also that in comparison to other psychological entities, ψυχή in Homer generally becomes active at the moment of loss of consciousness/death. Also see Darcus *Glotta* (1979), 30–31:
  in Homer ψυχή does not function as a psychic organ in man but seems simply to be the breath-soul endowing him with life. Only at the moment of death does ψυχή become prominent; once it has left the body it is active in its continued existence in the underworld.
[10] V 296; VIII 123, 315.
[11] Κεκαδών, connected possibly with χάζομαι, "reculer," Chantraine, 510–511, 1239.
[12] See Koch 1976 on the etymology of ὄλλυμι. Formally he has worked out a partially satisfactory explanation for the form of the verb; because of its connection with the Homeric formula αἰπὺς ὄλεθρος, however, it seems fairly certain that the verb means not "destroy" but, 218: "*(kill by) throw(ing) down a precipice', with active inflection, and, with middle desinences, *'(die by) fall(ing) from a precipice.'
[13] Schnaufer 1970, 199 note 540 on the readings ἀμπνύνθη, ἄμπνυτο at V 697 and XXII 475 respectively:
  Deshalb ist das besser überlieferte ἄμπνυτο bzw. ἀμπνύνθη der Lesart ἔμπνυτο bzw. ἐμπνύνθη vorzuziehen. Die Präposition ανα- ist eher geeignet, das Zurückkehren der Atmung, das Wiederaufatmen zu bezeichnen, als die Präposition ἐν-.
[14] A hopelessly awkward but accurate translation, offered with apologies.

of consciousness:

> ..... οὐδ' ἔτι κεῖτο, νέον δ' ἐσαγείρετο θυμόν,
>
> ..... nor was he still lying down, but he was gathering in anew his θυμός, ...

In the first two passages, θυμός returns as the revived person breathes again; and in the first, the North Wind assists in the revival. At XXII 475, the θυμός is gathered back into the φρήν as Andromakhe breathes again. Gathering occurs also at XV 240 when Hektor revives. Θυμός is connected in each case with the act of breathing, and/or movement into the φρήν implying return to a normal state, and/or the action of the wind.

§6. Ψυχή survives death: In continuing to examine the divergences between ψυχή, μένος, and θυμός in the subcontext of death, we find that ψυχή, and also μένος,[15] have associations very different from θυμός. Ψυχή survives death and goes to Hades.[16] Even when not yet in Hades, the ψυχή continues to exist after death as an entity, as at XXIII 100–101:

> ..... ψυχή δὲ κατὰ χθονὸς ἠΰτε καπνὸς
> ᾤχετο τετριγυῖα· ....
>
> ..... but the ψυχή went, squeaking, like smoke, beneath the earth; .....

Akhilleus exclaims, after the apparition has departed, that there is indeed a ψυχή and an εἴδωλον in the house of Hades, that it has no φρένες, and that in this case it resembles the living Patroklos. In two other passages, Akhilleus speaks of the ψυχή being irrevocably lost to the person once it has left the body at death. At IX 318–322,

> ἴση μοῖρα μένοντι, καὶ εἰ μάλα τις πολεμίζοι·
> ἐν δὲ ἰῇ τιμῇ ἠμὲν κακὸς ἠδὲ καὶ ἐσθλός·
> κάτθαν' ὁμῶς ὅ τ' ἀεργὸς ἀνὴρ ὅ τε πολλὰ ἐοργώς.
> οὐδέ τί μοι περίκειται, ἐπεὶ πάθον ἄλγεα θυμῷ,
> αἰεὶ ἐμὴν ψυχὴν παραβαλλόμενος πολεμίζειν.

> The same fate comes to him who holds back and to him who fights; in equal τιμή are the coward and the brave man. Likewise, the man who has done nothing and the one who has accomplished much both die. Nor is there any profit for me, from the time when I suffered grief in my θυμός, always to fight, setting my ψυχή at hazard.

It is the loss of ψυχή which determines a man's death, the θυμός which experiences woe at the possibility. The same belief is expressed, also by Akhilleus, at IX 408–409:

> ἀνδρὸς δὲ ψυχὴν πάλιν ἐλθεῖν οὔτε λεϊστὴ
> οὔθ' ἑλετή, ἐπεὶ ἄρ κεν ἀμείψεται ἕρκος ὀδόντων.

---

[15] See Nagy 1980, 164, 184. Also cf. Schnaufer 1970, 201.
[16] VII 330, XVI 625.

But a man's ψυχή cannot be seized or taken to come back, when once it shall cross the barrier of the teeth.

§7. Manner of leaving the body: Despite the differences in how θυμός and ψυχή are treated upon final separation from the body, it should be noted that the manner of departure can be the same. Both are described as flying away, for example at XVI 856, when Patroklos dies:

ψυχὴ δ' ἐκ ῥεθέων πταμένη Ἄϊδόσδε βεβήκει,

but the ψυχή, having flown from the limbs, went to Hades.

And at XXIII 880:

ὠκὺς δ' ἐκ μελέων θυμὸς πτάτο, ...

and swiftly the θυμός flew from the limbs, ...[17]

§8. Manner, cont.: (Ἀπο)πέτομαι is used with both θυμός and ψυχή as the manner of moving[18] and is significant particularly because it occurs only twice with each. This usage of θυμός occurs in the context of the death of animals, as at XVI 468–469:

. . . . ὁ δ' ἔβραχε θυμὸν ἀΐσθων,
κὰδ' δὲ πέσ' ἐν κονίῃσι μακών, ἀπὸ δ' ἔπτατο θυμός.

He screamed, gasping out his θυμός, and fell full-length in the dust, and his θυμός flew away.

Again, at the death of an animal at XXIII 880 the same verb is used with θυμός. There may well be a reason, as Garland suggests,[19] that only θυμός is used to describe the death of animals. But more important here is the fact that both entities move in the same way.

§9. Summary of loss of consciousness/death: In summarizing the findings for the entire context of loss of consciousness/death, it can be seen that θυμός has a number of distinctive characteristics. In the case of temporary loss of consciousness, it alone returns, in contrast to ψυχή which leaves. In this subcontext, it demonstrates connections with breathing and flying, as does ψυχή. Its location in the state of consciousness is said to be in the φρήν.[20] When death is described, only ψυχή goes to Hades. At IX 318–322, it was noted that Akhilleus uses both terms but is very clear about the fact that the ψυχή is what is risked in battle and that the θυμός is only that which suffers over this risk while the individual is alive and conscious. At IX 408–409, he speaks of the departure of the ψυχή as irrevocable. Therefore,

---

17 Cf. XXII 467 and XXIII 100.
18 See Garland 1981, Table 7.
19 Garland 1981, 49.
20 See XXII 475.

despite their similarities, the three functional synonyms θυμός/μένος/ψυχή are actually somewhat specialized.[21] Ψυχή has associations with the underworld, and also, like θυμός, with the breath.[22] Θυμός may have associations with the underworld but very definitely is to be linked with the breath and with the winds.

§10. Physiology of θυμός: It would be an oversimplification to equate θυμός with the breath and have done with it. As Böhme noted, Homeric diction does not compartmentalize the physiological and the psychological. The semantics of the words φρήν/φρένες is a case in point: described sometimes as physical organs and sometimes as an important psychological entity, they have successfully resisted a satisfactory definition,[23] not infrequently because it is difficult for the researcher to grasp the necessary connection between the two modes of operation. Onians was able to think in these terms by using the comparative method, and Böhme recognized the problem intellectually; but they saw this connection as a result of the confusion in the "primitive" mind of the early Greeks. Θυμός presents a similar problem.[24] The importance of its absence at death strongly suggests connection with the breath, but also it seems to be a vital part of the personality of the individual, to the extent that at times its use is equivalent to that of a reflexive pronoun.[25] But first it will be necessary to examine further the physiological connections of θυμός, which are implicit in the language of epic.

§11. Physiology, cont.: Θυμός is mentioned a number of times as being affected positively by food and drink.[26] Of a meal, it is frequently said that:

δαίνυντ', οὐδέ τι θυμὸς ἐδεύετο δαιτὸς ἐΐσης.

..... they feasted, nor was the θυμός lacking a due share of the feast.

At XVII 225–226, Hektor says to his allies:

τὰ φρονέων δώροισι κατατρύχω καὶ ἐδωδῇ
λαούς, ὑμέτερον δὲ ἑκάστου θυμὸν ἀέξω.

---

[21] Nagy 1981.

[22] See Böhme, 22 and 124. The passage at VII 131, where θυμός goes to the Underworld, is anomalous.

[23] See Onians 1954, Chapter 2, for a discussion of the φρήν/φρένες and other organs of consciousness. Ireland and Steel, 187–189, find his definition unsatisfactory both on medical and on methodological grounds.

[24] Böhme, 2–11, argues rightly that certain words, φρένες among them, have both physical and psychological import, and that attempts to explain one as developing from the other have not been successful. He classifies θυμός as strictly psychological but also sees it as being connected with the breath, p. 23.

[25] See Nagy 1979, 136, 22n.2.

[26] I 468, 602; II 431; VI 320; ; XXIII 56. Böhme, 31 ff., discusses Odysseus' speech at XIX 160 ff., quoted below, with an explanation of its significance, that food is translated as it were directly into battle.

In turning such things over in my φρένες, I wear out my people (by extracting from them) gifts and food, but I increase the θυμός of each one of you.

The θυμός has an undeniable connection not just with the physical condition of the body but with material wealth in general. Odysseus makes a point of describing this connection in his image of the hungry warrior which is couched in advice to Akhilleus at XIX 160–170:

> ἀλλὰ πάσασθαι ἄνωχθι θοῆς ἐπὶ νηυσὶν Ἀχαιοὺς
> σίτου καὶ οἴνοιο· τὸ γὰρ μένος ἐστὶ καὶ ἀλκή.
> οὐ γὰρ ἀνὴρ πρόπαν ἦμαρ ἐς ἠέλιον καταδύντα
> ἄκμηνος σίτοιο δυνήσεται ἄντα μάχεσθαι·
> εἴ περ γὰρ θυμῷ γε μενοινάᾳ πολεμίζειν,
> ἀλλά τε λάθρη γυῖα βαρύνεται, ἠδὲ κιχάνει
> δίψα τε καὶ λιμός, βλάβεται δέ τε γούνατ' ἰόντι.
> ὃς δέ κ' ἀνὴρ οἴνοιο κορεσσάμενος καὶ ἐδωδῆς
> ἀνδράσι δυσμενέεσσι πανημέριος πολεμίζῃ,
> θαρσαλέον νύ οἱ ἦτορ ἐνὶ φρεσίν, οὐδέ τι γυῖα
> πρὶν κάμνει, πρὶν πάντας ἐρωῆσαι πολέμοιο.

But bid the Achaians to take bread and wine beside the swift ships; for that is μένος and strength. A man will not be able to fight against (an adversary) all day long until sunset without food; even if in his θυμός he is eager to fight, yet secretly his limbs grow heavy, and hunger and thirst catch up with him, and his knees are impeded as he moves. But the man who is sated with wine and food may fight the enemy all day, and his ἦτορ in his φρένες is courageous, nor do his limbs grow weary before all have given ground.

Here the purely physical is opposed to the θυμός which is eager to fight despite lack of food. And yet it can be said, according to this passage, that the θυμός of an unfed man is not strong enough to carry on the battle. In light of the preceding passage in this section, θυμός increases and decreases. Consider in this connection Hephaistos' story of how Zeus, in a rage, hurled him from Mt. Olympus, and when he landed "there was little θυμός in me." In sum, these passages show that θυμός decreases in direct relation to the conditions existing in the body.

§12. Physiology, cont.: φρήν/φρένες: The absolutely vital link in this relation of θυμός to the body is the φρήν/φρένες. In the context of death, the θυμός disappears and the φρήν/φρένες also cease to exist:

> ὢ πόποι, ἦ ῥά τις ἐστι καὶ εἰν Ἀΐδαο δόμοισι
> ψυχὴ καὶ εἴδωλον, ἀτὰρ φρένες οὐκ ἔνι πάμπαν·[27]

Alas, there is indeed in the house of Hades a ψυχή and an image, but there are no φρένες in it at all.

But in a living body, the φρένες are present in the physical sense:

> ..... τοῦ δ' οὐχ ἅλιον βέλος ἔκφυγε χειρός

---

[27] XXIII 103–104. Also see x 493.

ἀλλ' ἔβαλ' ἔνθ ἄρα τε φρένες ἔρχαται ἀμφ' ἀδινὸν κῆρ.[28]

..... nor did the shaft leave his hand in vain, but he cast it where the φρένες come around the soft heart.

And then a few lines later, at XVI 503–504:

.... ὁ δὲ λὰξ ἐν στήθεσι βαίνων
ἐκ χροὸς ἕλκε δόρυ, προτὶ δὲ φρένες αὐτῷ ἕποντο·

.... and putting his heel to the chest, he drew the spear out of his body, and the φρένες followed it.

It cannot be argued convincingly that the ancient Greeks had no knowledge of anatomy, since experiences of this sort must have been commonplace at least for the male fighting population. And there was not only the battlefield: the need to slaughter animals for food would have acquainted almost everyone with the basic facts about anatomy. It must be admitted, therefore, that the description of the φρένες in relation to the heart is based on at least a crude observation.[29]

§13. Physiology, cont.: At XVI 481, the φρένες are said to surround the heart. This motion in repeated in a number of passages, with πόνος at VI 355, ἔρως at III 442 and XIV 294 both in conjunction with the verb ἀμφικαλύπτω; and in several pasages describing the filling of a person's φρένες with μένος, σθένος, and/or ἀλκή the preposition used is again ἀμφι.[30] Although θυμός and φρήν/φρένες so often occur together, and even are found in parallel construction, θυμός does not receive the same spatial treatment. For example, at XXII 312–313 θυμός occurs in the accusative with no preposition:

ὁρμήθη δ' 'Αχιλεύς, μένεος δ' ἐμπλήσατο θυμὸν
ἀγρίου, ...

Akhilleus attacked, and he was filled as to his θυμός with wild μένος, ...

Inherent in this difference of treatment is a different way of visualizing the φρένες as opposed to the θυμός.

§14. Physiology as indicated by adjectives: The respective adjectives used to describe φρένες and θυμός also give very distinct impressions of quality. The φρένες are described as μέλαιναι, πυκιναί, and ἔμπεδοι, among others; all these adjectives suggest a solidity not characteristic of θυμός.[31] Πυκινός, translated both as "close-knit" and as "clever, intelligent," is used at XVI

---

[28] XVI 480–481.
[29] See Onians, 35 ff. And Cheyns' article on the φρένες presents a thorough summary of post-classical definitions together with a rudimentary medical explanation of the possibilities.
[30] I 103–104, XVII 498–499, 573.
[31] See Onians 1954, 23–25.

212 to describe stones set closely together, at XII 57 of palisades, at X 267 of a house, and at XII 454 of a gate. It is used only rarely with φρήν/φρένες, as at XIV 294 (§13). The adverb πύκα᾽ used with verbs of construction to describe density of texture,[32] occurs with φρονέω to descirbe the nature of mental activity[33] and serves as an expression synonymous with πυκιναὶ φρένες. The internal act of taking care, of paying close attention, leads to a carefully-made structure or a well-constructed thought. The epithet πυκινός then is transferred from the organ of mental activity, from the mental action itself, and ultimately from the concrete result of an action, to the result of a mental activity, as at VI 187:

τῷ δ᾽ ἄρ᾽ ἀνερχομένῳ πυκινὸν δόλον ἄλλον ὕφαινε·

He wove another πυκινός trick for him on his arrival; . . . . .

In this particular passage, the verb ὑφαίνω heightens the importance of density of texture in relation to the activity of the φρήν/φρένες and the results of that activity. It should also be noted that πυκινός is used of βουλή at II 55, X 302; of νόος at XV 461, of ἔπος at VII 375, XI 788 and XXIV 75 and 744; and of μήδεα at III 202 and 208, and XXIV 282 and 674. It is also used of ἄτη at XXIV 480 and ἄχος at XVI 599.

§15. Physiology as indicated by adjectives, cont.: The φρένες are ἔμπεδοι when in a positive condition; thus it is that the φρένες of Paris, the "flighty" one of the *Iliad*, are described at VI 352-353 as follows:

τούτῳ ὁ᾽ οὔτ᾽ ἄρ᾽ νῦν φρένες ἔμπεδοι, οὔτ᾽ ἄρ᾽ ὀπίσσω ἔσσονται· . . . .

But his φρένες are not solid, nor will they be later, ...

At III 108, the φρένες of young men are referred to as being blown about:

αἰεὶ δ᾽ ὁπλοτέρων ἀνδρῶν φρένες ἠερέθονται·

But always the φρένες of younger men are blown about; . . . . .

The φρένες of the seer Teiresias, however, are described as ἔμπεδοι even in Hades, where ordinarily the φρένες are said no longer to exist.[34]

§16. Physiology as indicated by adjectives, cont.: The φρένες in a negative state are also described as λευγαλέοι. The etymology of this word is not entirely certain; but according to Chantraine, a more precise meaning may be at the root of the usual translation "wretched:" ...mais la famille est

---

[32] Chantraine, 953: "'de façon serrée, solide,'dit notamment d'objets, de constructions, aussi 'de façon serrée, précise' avec le verbe φρονέω." Note passages where it is used with βάλλομαι at IX 584, θωρήσσω at XII 317, XV 689 and 739, ἀραρίσκω at XII 454, ποιέω at XVIII 607.
[33] IX 554, XIV 217.
[34] XXIII 103-104, x. 493.

bien attestée, notamment en lat. avec *lūgeō* "être en deuil" (plus *lūctus*, *lugubris*), qui pourrait être le dénominatif d'un **lūgus*, i.e. **lougos* thématique, à côté d'un neutre sigmatique **λεῦγος (?). Les mots latins s'appliquent beaucoup plus précisément que les mots grecs à la manifestation violente de deuil, ce qui permet le rattachement de cette famille de mots a des termes comme skr. *rujáti* "briser" et *láuźti* "se briser" et *lúźti* "se briser", irl. *lucht* "portion", etc.[35]

It may be advisable in this case to give credence to the concrete meaning behind the more usual, and more figurative one; for it could be older. In this case, λευγαλέος is directly opposed to the favorable, or πυκινός state of the φρένες, as for example at IX 119-120:

ἀλλ' ἐπεὶ ἀασάμην φρεσὶ λευγαλέῃσι πιθήσας,
ἂψ ἐθέλω ἀρέσαι δόμεναί τ' ἀπερείσι' ἄποινα.

But since I was in error from trusting my λευγαλέαι φρένες, I am willing to make atonement and to give unlimited gifts.

§17. Physiology as indicated by adjectives, cont.: Θυμός, on the other hand, is never described as something even remotely solid, unless it is being described as abnormal. Akhilleus is accused a number of times for having an excessivley unyeileding θυμός, even more so than the gods, as for example at IX 496-498:

ἀλλ', 'Αχιλεῦ, δάμασον θυμὸν μέγαν· οὐδέ τί σε χρὴ
νηλεὲς ἦτορ ἔχειν· στρεπτοὶ δέ τε καὶ θεοὶ αὐτοί,
τῶν περ καὶ μείζων ἀρετὴ τιμή τε βίη τε.

But Akhilleus, master your great θυμός; it is not required that you have a pitiless ἦτορ; even the gods themselves can be moved, they whose excellence and honor and might are greater.

The adjective στρεπτός can be connected with θυμός by implication in this passage, since the inflexibility of the θυμός and the ἦτορ is contrasted directly to the nature of the gods, which is flexible. A little further on, the unfortunate characteristics of his θυμός are described overtly, at IX 636-638:

..........σοὶ δ' ἄλληκτόν τε κακόν τε
θυμὸν ἐνὶ στήθεσσι θεοὶ θέσαν εἵνεκα κούρη
οἴης·..........

..........and the gods put an unceasing and evil θυμός in your chest on account of one girl;..........

And at XXII 357 Hektor says to Akhilleus:

..........ἦ γὰρ σοί γε σιδήρεος ἐν φρεσὶ θυμός.

---

[35] Chantraine, 632.

.... indeed the θυμός in your φρένες is of iron.

The quality of being unchanging or unyielding could be called the negative aspect of being steadfast, or ἔμπεδος, which as we saw in §15 is a positive way of describing the φρένες. Therefore, although it would be impossible to prove in relation to θυμός that the modifiers discussed cannot be understood synchronically as somewhat metaphorical at the very least, it is indisputable that diachronically θυμός and φρένες were visualized as having different natures.

§18. Connection between physiology and psychology: In short, epic diction makes a connection between the physical nature of θυμός and its role in the psychology of the individual. We have seen that it leaves the body at death, permanently; and that its temporary absence determines syncope, its return revival. In both cases, it can, although it does not always, depart with a gasp, flutter, or waft away. It is affected by the needs and condition of the body, benefitting from food and rest and suffering from neglect or injury. A θυμός deprived of the necessities is of little support to its owner. Likewise, a θυμός which for any reason has acquired undesirable physical/metaphorical characteristics impedes the proper behavior of the person it inhabits, the θυμός of Akhilleus being the case in point. After this discussion of the role of the θυμός in the primarily physical life of the individual, its role in the cognitive context will be taken up. And since epic diction does not compartmentalize the psychological and the physical, there is here also a physical aspect to be considered.

§19. Cognition: In fact, this relationship between the physical and the psychological is particularly evident in the context of cognition. The adjective πεπνυμένος[36] is used frequently in the *Odyssey* to describe an idea which is sound or well thought-out. To cite only one of many examples, at i 361 (= xxi 355):

παιδὸς γὰρ μῦθον πεπνυμένον ἔνθετο θυμῷ.

..... she put her son's πεπνυμένος speech into her θυμός.

At V 696–698, it was seen that Sarpedon returns to consciousness with the help of the North Wind. Therefore, even if an indisputable etymological connection cannot be made between πνείω and πεπνύμαι, a thematic connection already exists: the result of breathing is consciousness, which necessarily has a relationship to intelligence.[37]

---

[36] Chantraine, 883–884, would prefer not to make a direct etymological connection.
[37] See Jean-Paul Vernant, *Mythe et Pensée ches les Grecs* 1, 95–96:
On connaît, de reste, les liens qui unissent, dans la pensée grecque archaïque, l'âme et le souffle respiratoire. Les formules de Platon sur l'âme se ramassant en elle-même à partir de tous les points du corps évoquent cette croyance, partagée, selon

§20. Cognition, cont.: Andromakhe's revival from a fainting spell at XXII 475 was mentioned in §5 in connection with the divergence between ψυχή and θυμός. The passage is particularly relevant because the verb ἄμπνυτο is virtually synonymous with the phrase ἐς φρένα θυμὸς ἀγέρθη; θυμός, therefore, is connected both with the breath and with consciousness. But note also that the act of breathing brings the θυμός back into the φρήν, a functional synonym particularly in this context. In §15–§17, adjectives modifying φρήν/φρένες were discussed in order to explore its/their nature. The location of this organ is given occasionally as or is implied to be the στῆθος/στήθεα, which is frequently given as the location of the θυμός.[38] For instance, at XVII 469–470, Automedon's φρένες in his στήθεα have been replaced by a poor idea:

> Αὐτόμεδον, τίς τοί νυ θεῶν νηκερδέα βουλὴν
> ἐν στήθεσσιν ἔθηκε, καὶ ἐξέλετο φρένας ἐσθλάς;

Automedon, which of the gods put this profitless plan in your chest and took away your good φρένες?

§21. Cognition, cont.: Since the connection of both θυμός and φρήν/φρένες with the breath has been discussed briefly, it is necessary to continue by examining θυμός in the context of cognition *per se*. Θυμός is not used frequently in this context. Its functional synonyms are νόος, νόημα, φρήν, φρένες, and κραδίη; and it is used with the verbs μανθάνω, οἶδα, φρονέω, φράζω, νοέω, and γιγνώσκω to describe intelligence. The verbs ἀάζω and θέλγω are used to describe lack of intelligence.

§22. Cognition, cont.: A thought-provoking passage in this connection is Hektor's moving speech at VI 441–446:

> ἦ καὶ ἐμοὶ τάδε πάντα μέλει, γύναι· ἀλλὰ μάλ' αἰνῶς
> αἰδέομαι Τρῶας καὶ Τρῳάδας ἑλκεσιπέπλους,
> αἴ κε κακὸς ὣς νόσφιν ἀλυσκάζω πολέμοιο·
> οὐδέ με θυμὸς ἄνωγεν, ἐπεὶ μάθον ἔμμεναι ἐσθλὸς
> αἰεὶ καὶ πρώτοισι μετὰ Τρώεσσι μάχεσθαι,
> ἀρνύμενος πατρός τε μέγα κλέος ἠδ' ἐμὸν αὐτοῦ.

All these things are concerns to me, lady; but I should feel dreadfully ashamed before the Trojans and the Trojan women of the trailing robes if, like a coward, I should shrink from battle. Nor does my θυμός bid me, since I have learned to be noble and always to fight in the Trojan front ranks, winning great reknown for my father and for myself.

The expression οὐδέ με θυμός ἄνωγεν is a negative expression of motivation

---

Aristote, par les Orphiques, que l'âme est dispersée à travers le corps dans lequel elle s'est introduite, portée par les vents, pendant la respiration.

[38] It would be excessive to cite all the examples, for there are many; but here is a partial list from the *Iliad*: IV 313, 360; V 317, 346; VII 216, 349, 369; VIII 6; IX 629, 637; XIII 73, XVI 503–504, and so on. Στῆθος/στήθεα as the location of the θυμός is on a par with φρήν/φρένες.

resulting from Hektor's education in the line of duty. This passage is unusual in that θυμός is so often the psychic entity which is uppermost at moments of impulse, whether implied or overt. But the fact that Hektor's motivation is expressed in a manner atypical of epic diction is an important indication of the difference between his character and that of Akhilleus, a difference which probably extends back into the prehistory of the Homeric poems.[39] More important, this atypicality should not be taken as underlying insignificance; rather, its presence in this passage not only confirms its role in this context but is an indication that important decisions are seen to have an emotional aspect.

§23. Cognition, cont.: Akhilleus is described quite differently at XXIV 39–43:

ἀλλ' ὀλοῷ Ἀχιλῆϊ, θεοί, βούλεσθ' ἐπαρήγειν,
ᾧ οὔτ' ἄρ φρένες εἰσὶν ἐναίσιμοι οὔτε νόημα
γναμπτὸν ἐνὶ στήθεσσι, λέων δ' ὣς ἄγρια οἶδεν,
ὅς τ' ἐπεὶ ἄρ μεγάλῃ τε βίῃ καὶ ἀγήνορι θυμῷ
εἴξας εἶσ' ἐπὶ μῆλα βροτῶν, ἵνα δαῖτα λάβῃσιν:

But, gods, you wish to help baneful Akhilleus, whose φρένες are not just and whose νόημα in his chest cannot be bent, since he knows wild things like a lion, who, having yielded to his great force and his mighty θυμός, will attack men's flocks in order to seize a feast; . . . . .

Akhilleus is compared to a lion who yields to his θυμός; he is a wild animal who has no control over his impulses. The passage emphasizes this side of his nature by endowing him with unjust φρένες and an unbending νόημα: his impulse of the moment is all that matters. He is fierce rather than brave out of a sense of duty; whereas personal affection might restrain Hektor, it stimulates Akhilleus' lust for battle. Because of what has already been said about him, it is known that his θυμός is κακός, ἄλληκτος, and σιδήρεος, all undesirable qualities in this psychological entity. Hence his cognitive functions are adversely affected.[40]

§24. Cognition, cont.: Perception of the future occurs in the θυμός along with other organs of cognition. At VI 447–449, Hektor prophesies the fall of Troy:

εὖ γὰρ ἐγὼ τόδε οἶδα κατὰ φρένα καὶ κατὰ θυμόν·
ἔσσεται ἦμαρ ὅτ' ἄν πότ' ὀλώλῃ Ἴλιος ἱρή
καὶ Πρίαμος καὶ λαὸς ἐϋμμελίω Πριάμοιο.

For I know this well in my φρήν and in my θυμός; there will be a day when sacred Ilion will perish, and Priam and the host of Priam of the goodly ashen spear.

---

[39] See Nagy 1979, 324.
[40] Nagy, 1979, 135.

At XII 228–229, the θυμός of the seer perceives the meanings of the signs:

ὧδέ χ' ὑποκρίναιτο θεοπρόπος, ὃς σάφα θυμῷ
εἰδείη τεράων καί οἱ πειθοίατο λαοί.

And thus a seer would answer, who perceived the omens clearly in his θυμός and in whom the host would trust.

Inability to see the future is expressed in slightly different terms at I 342–344:

..... ἦ γὰρ ὅ γ' ὀλοιῇσι φρεσὶ θύει,
οὐδέ τι οἶδε νοῆσαι ἅμα πρόσσω καὶ ὀπίσσω,
ὅππως οἱ παρὰ νηυσὶ σόοι μαχέοιντο 'Αχαιοί.

..... for he is raging in his deadly φρένες, nor does he know how to see ahead and behind at the same time, how the Akhaians may fight in safety beside the ships.

The turmoil of the φρένες, designated with the verb θύω, prevents Agamemnon, according to Akhilleus, from having a clear perception of the past and the future. The wording of 342 is reminiscent of the phrase θυμός ἐνὶ φρεσί and suggests that after all the θυμός is present but in an agitated condition.[41]

§25. Cognition, cont.: Additional passages demonstrate that there is little uniformity in how θυμός is used in the context of cognition. At II 408–409, Menelaos perceives his brother's feelings with his θυμός:

αὐτόματος δέ οἱ ἦλθε βοὴν ἀγαθὸς Μενέλαος·
ᾔδεε γὰρ κατὰ θυμὸν ἀδελφεὸν ὡς ἐπονεῖτο.

And of his own accord, Menelaos of the goodly shout came to him; for he knew in his brotherly θυμός how he (Agamemnon) was suffering.

Synonymity between οἶδα κατὰ θυμόν and φρονέω is implied by the following passage at IV 360–361:

οἶδα γὰρ ὥς τοι θυμὸς ἐνὶ στήθεσσι φίλοισιν
ἤπια δήνια οἶδε· τὰ γὰρ φρονέεις ἅ τ' ἐγώ περ.

For I know how your θυμός in your dear breast knows favorable plans; for you have the understanding I have.

The last half of 361 is virtually a gloss of the preceding line and a half. Another relevant passage occurs in Diomedes' description of Odysseus at X 244–247:

οὗ πέρι μὲν πρόφρων κραδίη καὶ θυμὸς ἀγήνωρ
ἐν πάντεσσι πόνοισι, φιλεῖ δέ ἑ Παλλὰς 'Αθήνη.

---

[41] Darcus 1979, 166, concludes that in general the φρήν/φρένες and the person cooperate, that conflict tends to occur more often between the individual and his other psychic organs, e.g. the θυμός.

τούτου γ' έσπομένοιο καὶ ἐκ πυρὸς αἰθομένοιο
ἄμφω νοστήσαιμεν, ἐπεὶ περίοιδε νοῆσαι.

..... whose eager heart and manly θυμός excel in all sorts of trials, and Pallas Athene loves him. If he were to go with me, we should both return even out of blazing fire, since he excels in the use of his νόος.

Here the heart and the θυμός of Odysseus are equated with his νόος, as in the previous passage the knowing θυμός is equated with the activity of the φρήν/φρένες. If the wording is to be taken at face value, it appears that the activity νοεῖν takes place in the θυμός. Odysseus is traditionally the man of νόος/νόστος and also the one who returns by means of his νόος,[42] a fact which is emphasized by the wording of this passage. The fact that θυμός is mentioned here particularly indicates again that its use in the context of cognition is a well-grounded fact.

At xv 211–212, θυμός and φρήν occur with οἶδα in a line familiar from VI 447:

εὖ γὰρ ἐγὼ τόδε οἶδα κατὰ φρένα καὶ κατὰ θυμόν,
οἷος κείνου θυμὸς ὑπέρβιος· . . . .

For I know this in my φρήν and in my θυμός, how proud his θυμός is; . . . .

Here both θυμός and φρήν are involved in the perception of the nature of another person's θυμός, perception, in other words, on a rather sophisticated level. The use of θυμός in the context of cognition thus raises the question of whether cognition itself can be considered simply an intellectual activity, or whether at times it contains elements of emotion.[43]

It can be seen, in summarizing this section, that the verb οἶδα expresses perception in respect to θυμός, φρήν/φρένες, κραδίη, and νόος. There is also in three out of the four passages an emotional element independent of the word θυμός. There are thus two possible answers to the question of why θυμός is used at all in this context: either epic diction is somewhat

---

[42] See Frame 1978 for discussions on νόος/νόστος in relation to Odysseus. This passage is the important description of Odysseus' nature as linked with his destiny.

[43] E. L. Harrison, 1960, 71:
We have noted already that the dividing lines between various types of mental activity in Homer are blurred. Thus thought tends to be worried thought, angry thought, and so on. Hence, naturally enough, the θυμός is often involved in activity of this sort: indeed, it is the main locus of Homeric man's deliberation and decision, especially when this involves him in a monologue. It is therefore quite wrong to see the key to its Homeric usage in terms of the emotional to the exclusion of the rational, or even to try to explain away the rational element as if it were anomalous. In fact, the Homeric θυμός is so impoprtant in this field that later on, when θυμός and its compounds are generally put in antithesis with the reason, ἐνθυμεῖσθαι can nevertheless describe rational activity (e.g. Thuc. 8.68) and ἐνθύμημα can be a technical term for a logical process (*LSJ, s.v.*). Both these words recall a common Homeric usage of θυμός that has meanwhile disappeared.

indiscriminate in its choice of language pertaining to inner processes, and in particular mental activity; or there is a more subtle reason for the choice of certain words, in particular of θυμός, to describe nuances of inner experience. This question will be discussed again once all the material on θυμός in the context of cognition has been examined.

§26. Cognition: νοέω In the preceding pages, it was seen that the activity νοεῖν could take place in the θυμός. This combination occurs again at xviii 228–230; it is not absolutely clear whether the verb οἶδα is intended to be a restatement of the whole phrase θυμῷ νοέω or simply an amplification of νοέω

αὐτὰρ ἐγὼ θυμῷ νοέω καὶ οἶδα ἕκαστα,
ἐσθλά τε καὶ τὰ χέρεια· πάρος δ' ἔτι νήπιος ἦα.
ἀλλά τοι οὐ δύναμαι πεπνυμένα πάντα νοῆσαι·

..... but I use my νόος in my θυμός and perceive each thing, the noble and the worse; formerly I was still a child. But I am not able to perceive all πεπνυμένα things; .....

In either case, it is clear that perception again takes place in the θυμός. The opposing condition is that of childishness, the inability to perceive the relative merit of things. In the last line, Telemakhos qualifies his abilities: his perceptions are keener than they used to be but not totally dependable in relation to πεπνυμένα.[44] At XXIV 376–377, however, Priam has no such reservations when he says to Akhilleus:

..... οἷος δὴ σὺ δέμας καὶ εἶδος ἀγητός,
πέπνυσαί τε νόῳ, μακάρων δ' ἔξ ἐσσι τοκήων.

..... for you are admirable in form and beauty and πέπνυσαι in your νόος, and you are the son of blessed parents.

It is helpful to find the phrase πέπνυσαι νόῳ in the *Iliad*, providing an equivalent to the use of πεπνυμένος which is so common in the *Odyssey*, for it is possible to assume that the latter participle refers to the proper use of the νόος, even when not overt as at xviii 230. And νόος as we have seen, has associations with θυμός in the diction of both epics within the context of cognition.

§27. Cognition: νοέω cont.: Νοέω is used with the phrase κατὰ φρένα καὶ κατὰ θυμὸν at XX 262–266:

.... φάτο γὰρ δολιχόσκιον ἔγκος
ῥέα διελεύσεσθαι μεγαλήτορος Αἰνείαο,
νήπιος, οὐδ' ἐνόησε κατὰ φρένα καὶ κατὰ θυμὸν
ὡς οὐ ῥηΐδι' ἐστὶ θεῶν ἐρικυδέα δῶρα
ἀνδράσι γε θνητοῖσι δαμήμεναι οὐδ' ὑποείκειν.

---

[44] Cf. xxi. 343, 355; also 19.

.... for he thought that the long-shadowed spear of great-hearted Aineias would easily go through, fool, nor did he perceive in his φρήν and his θυμός how the glorious works of the gods are not easy for men to overcome and do not yield to them.

This passage is identical in construction with passages discussed above in §24, where the phrase κατὰ φρένα καὶ κατὰ θυμόν is used with the verb οἶδα. In the context of θυμός and φρήν, therefore, οἶδα works as a functional synonym of νοέω.

And to emphasize further the importance of θυμός in the act of cognition, it is found in parallel construction with νόος at IV 308–309:

ὧδε καὶ οἱ πρότεροι πόλεας καὶ τείχε' ἐπόρθεον,
τόνδε νόον καὶ θυμὸν ἐνὶ στήθεσσιν ἔχοντες.

for thus the men of olden times used to sack cities and strongholds, having νόος and θυμός in their breasts.

Then the νόος is located in the θυμός at xiv 490–491:

ὣς ἐφάμην· ὁ δ' ἔπειτα νόον σχέθε τόνδ' ἐνὶ θυμῷ,
οἷος κεῖνος ἔην βουλευέμεν ἠδὲ μάχεσθαι· .....

Thus I spoke; but he had this sort of νόος in his θυμός, for he was the sort of man to plan and to fight; .....

It is undeniable that there is a connection between νόος and θυμός; the difficulty is in discovering the nature of the connection, since the relationship is expressed in several different ways, and since there are not enough passages in which both occur to be able to state on the basis of numbers which relationship was preferred by epic diction. All we can see from these few passages is that the νόος is more often located in the θυμός. There is also a connection between νοέω and θυμός and in this case again θυμός is the location of the activity.

§28. Cognition: γιγνώσκω: θυμός is rarely used with γιγνώσκω;[45] in both instances in the *Iliad*, there is some question as to whether θυμός cannot be connected with the subsequent emotion described. At XVI 119–120, Ajax suddenly recognizes the role of the gods in the current battle:

γνῶ δ' Αἴας κατὰ θυμὸν ἀμύμονα, ῥίγησέν τε,
ἔργα θεῶν, ὅ ῥα πάγχυ μάχης ἐπὶ μήδεα κεῖρε
Ζεὺς ὑψιβρεμέτης, Τρώεσσι δὲ βούλετο νίκην·

And Ajax recognized in his blameless θυμός and shuddered at the works of the gods, and the fact that Zeus the high-thundering entirely cut across his plans.

Θυμός seems here to refer primarily to the act of recognition, but it is possible to extend its range and to understand it as the location of the

---

[45] See Nagy *Arethusa* 1983, 36 ff.

subsequent emotion. A similar passage occurs at VII 189, where it seems clear that θυμός should be read only with γηθέω:

γνῶ δὲ κλήρου σῆμα ἰδών, γήθησε δέ θυμῷ.

Seeing the sign of the lot, he recognized it (,) and rejoiced in his θυμός.

The punctuation notwithstanding, θυμός is placed at the end of the line and separated from the verb of recognition by the participial phrase σῆμα ἰδών.[46] Nevertheless, the fact that it is used here indicates that it was seen as being appropriate to expressions of recognition, and also that acts of cognition are seen in epic diction overtly to be connected with the emotional function. The wording of XVI 530 further supports this view:

Γλαῦκος δ' ἔγνω ᾗσιν ἐνὶ φρεσὶ γήθησέν τε,

Glaukos knew in his φρένες and rejoiced, ...

Although here both the intellectual and the emotional actions take place in the φρένες, φρένες as location is synonymous with θυμός as location; and θυμός, as has been seen particularly in the subcontext of recovery from loss of consciousness, belongs in the φρένες.

§29. Cognition: φρονέω: Θυμός is found frequently as the location of the verb φρονέω formed on the root *phren/phron*, on which φρήν and perhaps φράζω are also formed. This collocation of words seems to be purely cognitive. Understandably, φρονέω is not found with its corresponding noun but with θυμός, which would have sounded less redundant but also enjoys partial synonymity with φρήν/φρένες. Τὰ φρονέοντ' ἀνὰ θυμὸν occurs at II 36 and XVIII 4; at VIII 430 the phrase φρονέων ἐνὶ θυμῷ is used.

§30. Cognition: φράζω: Θυμός occurs, in conjunction with φρήν/φρένες, with the verb φράζω, which may be connected etymologically with the same root *phren/phron* and which is definitely related semantically.[47] Like φρονέω, φράζω/φράζομαι denotes a mental process, such as that required to construct an intelligent plan. At XV 162–166, Zeus warns in his message to Poseidon that his brother should consider carefully the consequences of disobedience:

εἰ δέ μοι οὐκ ἐπέεσσ' ἐπιπείσεται, ἀλλ' ἀλογήσει,
φραζέσθω δὴ ἔπειτα κατὰ φρένα καὶ κατὰ θυμόν,
μή μ' οὐδὲ κρατερός περ ἐὼν ἐπιόντα ταλάσσῃ
μεῖναι, ἐπεί ἕο φημὶ βίῃ πολὺ φέρτερος εἶναι
καὶ γενεῇ πρότερος· . . . .

But if he will not be persuaded by my words, but disregards them, let him then consider carefully in his φρήν and his θυμός that he might not endure my

---

[46] Nagy, 1983 38 f.
[47] Chantraine 1225; Detienne/Vernant 1974 (English translation 1978), 23 n. 3.

attack, although he is strong, since I claim to be far stronger in force and the elder by birth.

Careful thought or deliberation is further suggested at XVI 646–647 by the use of μερμηρίζω:

ἀλλὰ κατ' αὐτοὺς αἰὲν ὅρα καὶ φράζετο θυμῷ,
πολλὰ μάλ' ἀμφὶ φόνῳ Πατρόκλου μερμηρίζων,

. . . . . but he looked down on them and considered many things in his θυμός, debating many things about the death of Patroklos, ...

At i 293–296, Athene recommends careful consideration to Telemakhos for the purpose of arriving at a plan:

αὐτὰρ ἐπὴν δὴ ταῦτα τελευτήσῃς τε καὶ ἔρξῃς,
φράζεσθαι δὴ ἔπειτα κατὰ φρένα καὶ κατὰ θυμὸν
ὅππως κε μνηστῆρας ἐνὶ μεγάροισι τεοῖσι
κτείνῃς ἠὲ δόλῳ ἢ ἀμφαδόν . . . .

But when you have finished and done with these things, consider then in your φρήν and in your θυμός how you may kill the suitors in your halls, whether by treachery or openly.

At IX 421–423, Akhilleus tells the embassy that the chiefs of the Akhaians need to come up with a better μῆτις:

ἀλλ' ὑμεῖς μὲν ἰόντες ἀριστήεσσιν Ἀχαιῶν
ἀγγελίην ἀπόφασθε – τὸ γὰρ γέρας ἐστὶ γερόντων –
ὄφρ' ἄλλην φράζωνται ἐνὶ φρεσὶ μῆτιν ἀμείνω, ...

But you, go back to the chiefs of the Akhaians and deliver this message — for this is the prerogative of the elders — that they should devise another better counsel in their φρένες, ...

Here again, the φρήν/φρένες are the location of the activity, and are preferred to θυμός as the location. Epic diction does in general prefer φρήν/φρένες in this context; therefore, it is to be expected that θυμός would not be used frequently in this word combination.

§31. Cognition: βουλή, "plan," shows little marked preference for either θυμός or φρήν/φρένες, except for the fact that it occurs a number of times in the formulaic line:

ἥδε δέ οἱ κατὰ θυμὸν ἀρίστη φαίνετο βουλή,[48]

But this plan appeared best to him in his θυμός, ...

At XX 20, Zeus says to Poseidon:

ἔγνως, ἐννοσίγαιε, ἐμὴν ἐν στήθεσι βουλήν,

---

[48] Cf. II 5, X 17, XIV 161, ix 318, xi 424, *H.Ven.* 235.

Earth-shaker, you have learned the plan in my breast, ...

And at xiv 337–338, it is the φρένες which are affected:

..... τοῖσιν δὲ κακὴ φρεσὶν ἥνδανε βουλὴ
ἀμφ' ἐμοί, ὄφρ' ἔτι πάγχυ δύης ἐπὶ πῆμα γενοίμην.

..... a base plan in their φρένες concerning me gave pleasure, that I might still come upon any evil suffering at all.

In this context, therefore, θυμός/φρήν/φρένες/στήθεα are functional synonyms.

§32. Cognition: μήδομαι, μήδεα: In combination with μήδομαι, "I devise," the location if specified is generally in the φρένες, as at XXI 19 = XXIII 176:

.... κακὰ δὲ φρεσὶ μήδετο ἔργα,

.... and he was devising base deeds in his φρένες, ...

Only at VI 157 does the devising take place in the θυμός:

..... αὐτάρ οἱ Προῖτος κακὰ μήσατο θυμῷ,

..... but Proitos was devising base things in his θυμός,

Usage with μήδεα also shows a preference for the φρένες, as at XVII 325 and at XXIV 673–674. The latter passage is particularly interesting:[49]

οἱ μὲν ἄρ' ἐν προδόμῳ δόμου αὐτόθι κοιμήσαντο,
κῆρυξ καὶ Πρίαμος, πυκινὰ φρεσὶ μήδε' ἔχοντες.

They lay down there in the entryway of the house, the herald and Priam, having πυκινὰ μήδεα in their φρένες.

Either the plans are coming thick and fast, or they partake of the texture characteristic of the φρένες at their best (§14). And then at ii 37–38, although the location is not specified, we are reminded of the connection to the participle πεπνυμένος of both θυμός and φρήν/φρένες:[50]

.... σκῆπτρον δέ οἱ ἔμβαλε χειρὶ
κῆρυξ Πεισήνωρ, πεπνυμένα μήδεα εἰδώς.

And the herald Peisenor who knows πεπνυμένα counsels put the staff in his hand.

We have just seen that μήδεα are found in the φρένες; at xxi 343 (=355), a

---

[49] Cf. 14, also xi 445–446.

[50] Nagy 1974, 269–278, points out that the μήδεα of the gods are regularly called ἄφθιτα, while those of men, as we see above, are πεπνυμένα. If we consider again the questions raised in 15, the contrast between mortal and immortal intelligences may begin to seem entirely logical.

μῦθος πεπνυμένος is put by Penelope into her own θυμός. In this subcontext of μήδομαι/μήδεα, therefore, φρένες is preferred as the location. Θυμός is an alternative and also shares associations with the participle πεπνυμένος.

§33. Cognition: λανθάνω, οὐκ νοέω, ἀάζω: In the absence of appropriate intellectual functioning, θυμός and φρήν/φρένες are used, as are also νόος and νοέω. These expressions, which are varied but not numerous, take several different forms. At IX 533, Meleager's error in judgment is explained thus:[51]

ἢ λάθετ' ἢ οὐκ ἐνόησεν· ἀάσσατο δὲ μέγα θυμῷ.

Either he forgot, or he did not use his νόος; but he was greatly in error in his θυμός.

The parallel with Akhilleus is, of course, both intentional and ominous; the latent threat is there, both to Akhilleus' reputation as a leader of men, and to the beleaguered Greek army. Akhilleus' own θυμός is characterized later as ἄλληκτος, κακός, even σιδήρεος.[52] Meleager's failing in the θυμός is either the result of forgetfulness, or failure to use his νόος: both are very serious, as can be seen at xxi 301–302 in Antinoos' account of the battle of the Lapiths and the Centaurs and the madness of the Centaur Eurytion:

.... ὁ δὲ φρεσὶν ᾗσιν ἀασθεὶς
ἤϊεν ἣν ἄτην ὀχέων ἀεσίφρονι θυμῷ.

But he, erring in his φρένες, went enduring that harm with weakened θυμός.

This last passage has provided a wealth of material for an article on the etymology and semantics of ἄτη, ἀασάμην etc.[53] which will be discussed in the conclusion. Particularly important here is the fact that when the φρήν/-φρένες do not function properly, the θυμός is described as ἀεσίφρων, i.e. belonging to φρήν/φρένες which are blown about. As was mentioned in §15, airiness is for them an inappropriate quality.

It is explained a little later, at IX 549–550, why Meleager's νόος was not functioning:

ἀλλ' ὅτε δὴ Μελέαγρον ἔδυ χόλος, ὅς τε καὶ ἄλλων
οἰδάνει ἐν στήθεσσι νόον πύκα φρονεόντων,......[54]

But when anger came upon Meleager, anger which even swells the νόος in the breasts of those who use their φρένες carefully .....

The physical aspects of θυμός and φρήν/φρένες reappear here: the failure of

---

[51] Cf. *H. Dem.* 246, XI 340.
[52] IX 636–638, XXII 357.
[53] See E. D. Francis, 1983, especially 81–103.
[54] Cf. 14–16.

the intellect to function properly is put in physical terms.⁵⁵ The anger itself, or perhaps more appropriately the substance bile, becomes the agent which produces a physical effect upon the νόος. Therefore again the physical, the cognitive, and here even the emotional are intertwined.

§34. Cognition: φρένες, ἀάζομαι: In §14 and §15, it was noted that in order to function properly, the φρήν/φρένες should be close-knit and solid. At IX 119, Agamemnon describes his erroneous φρένες:⁵⁶

> ἀλλ' ἐπεὶ ἀασάμην φρεσὶ λευγαλέῃσι πιθήσας, ...
>
> But since I was greatly in error, having relied upon my wretched (torn?) φρένες, ...

Because of the repeated insistence in various passages on the importance of the physical state to mental and emotional functions, it is necessary at least to reconsider a more literal translation of λευγαλέος. The meaning "wretched" is vague in relation to the φρένες; to describe them as "torn," however, based on Chantraine's suggestion, is precisely to the point.

Similar language is used again at XIX 136–138, again by Agamemnon speaking of his treatment of Akhilleus:

> οὐ δυνάμην λελαθέσθ' Ἄτης, ᾗ πρῶτον ἀάσθην.
> ἀλλ' ἐπεὶ ἀασάμην καί μευ φρένας ἐξέλετο Ζεύς,
> ἂψ ἐθέλω ἀρέσαι, δόμεναί τ' ἀπερείσι' ἄποινα·
>
> . . . . . I was not able to be unmindful of Ἄτη, on account of whom I had erred first. But since I erred and (since) Zeus had taken away my φρένες, I wish to make recompense and to give unlimited compensation; . . . . .

Again, the failure to think properly is connected with the φρένες, this time with their absence. This passage is reminiscent of the forgetfulness of Meleager, and of the fact that the dead are said to have no φρένες.⁵⁷

§35. Cognition: θέλγω: The verb θέλγω is also used to describe the absence of intelligence and the temporary removal of good judgment by a divine agent, as for example at XV 321–322:

> . . . . τοῖσι δὲ θυμὸν
> ἐν στήθεσσιν ἔθελξε, λάθοντο δὲ θούριδος ἀλκῆς.
>
> . . . . and he charmed the θυμός in their breasts, and they forgot their rushing strength.

Again, at XV 593–595, Zeus gives μένος to the Trojans and simultaneously bewitches the Greeks:

---

⁵⁵ See 14–16.
⁵⁶ See 17.
⁵⁷ Cf. XXIII 104.

> .... Διὸς δέ τέλειον ἐφετμάς,
> ὅ σφισιν αἰὲν ἔγειρε μένος μέγα, θέλγε δὲ θυμὸν
> Ἀργείων καὶ κῦδος ἀπαίνυτο, τοὺς δ' ὀρόθυνεν.
>
> .... and they fulfilled the behests of Zeus, who kept awakening in them great μένος, but he kept bewitching the θυμός of the Argives and denying them glory and drove the others on.

In the first passage, the state of being bewitched in the θυμός is equated with being forgetful, in this case of one's ἀλκή. In the second passage, the enchantment of the θυμός in the Greeks is opposed to the awakening of μένος in the Trojans.[58] At XII 254–255, Zeus bewitches the νόος of the Greeks; and at xviii 212 and 282, Penelope with Athena's help bewitches the suitors.

§36. Cognition: presence of emotion: During the examination of θυμός in the context of the intellect, the question arose in §22–§25 and §27 as to whether it was present simply as a functional synonym of φρήν/φρένες/νόος or should indicate admixtures of feeling within the larger context of cognition. In §22 and §23, we saw that the respective θυμός of Hektor and of Akhilleus are motivated by education and by bestial impulses. In Hektor the θυμός has been taught impulses proper to social responsibility and respectability which override those arising from personal motives, i.e. feeling for Andromakhe. In Akhilleus the θυμός is lion-like and not to be turned from the course it is set on, any more than one can turn aside a lion from his purpose of finding food. The two passages taken together suggest that θυμός is not entirely synonymous with the intellect, although it functions at times in conjunction with it. It also seems that the intellect at times functions in ways conditioned by the nature of the θυμός in the individual.

In §25, all examples given also contain an emotional element: at II 409 and xv 211–212, the θυμός of the perceiver recognizes the nature of the emotion in another person; at IV 360–361, unanimity with another is expressed; and at X 244, Diomedes speaks of both Odysseus' κραδίη and his θυμός in the same breath. In §28, it seemed likely that both the verbs of perception and the verbs of emotion could be connected with θυμός. We have seen, therefore, that in a number of cases which were labelled cognitive or intellectual at the outset, for purposes of organization, have been found to be not simply that. Out of the rather infrequent occurrences of θυμός in this context, at least six can be connected with some element of emotion in the perceiver or the perceived. A sense of the workings of Homeric psychological vocabulary begins to emerge: θυμός is frequently present in such

---

[58] See Nagy 1974, 266–269, on μένος. Forgetfulness is essentially the opposite of being endowed with μένος.

passages for the purpose of indicating the simultaneous presence of emotion and cognition.

§37. Cognition: summary: Generally, therefore, we can still say that θυμός/φρήν/φρένες/νόος are functional synonyms in the context of cognition or intellect. But there is some differentiation. In collocation with φρονέω, it seems probable that θυμός was used to avoid redundancy. The fact that it is used at X 244–247 in the description of Odysseus indicates that it is an important element in a person's intellectual make-up. In six other passages, it is highly likely that θυμός indicated the presence of an emotional element within the function of cognition. Therefore, out of all twenty-three passages discussed, the use of θυμός may be required for reasons other than functional synonymity with φρήν/φρένες/νόος. As was true in the context of loss of consciousness/death, differentiation is evident but occurs side by side with functional synonymity.

§38. Emotion: Next we must examine θυμός in the context of emotions, where it occurs with the greatest frequency. It is the site of grief, fear, anxiety, hope, desire, love, anger, joy, delight, and so on. Its synonyms in this context are φρήν/φρένες, κῆρ, κραδίη and ἦτορ; and in a number of cases the prepositional phrases ἐνὶ φρεσί, μετὰ φρεσί and so on suggest its presence even when the word itself is not used.

Since verbs of emotion occur with great frequency unaccompanied by any psychological term, we can assume that the inclusion of θυμός or any of its synonyms was not vital to the sense. It is also inevitable, in accordance with what is known about the method of composition of the Homeric poems, that certain words and phrases were useful for filling out lines to which other words and phrases could not be adapted. It is unlikely, however, that metrical needs can explain the fact that the overall use of θυμός is twice as extensive that of φρήν/φρένες in this context. Χαίρω, for example, occurs twelve times with θυμός but only once with φρένες. And although the use of φρήν/φρένες is distributed fairly evenly between contexts of cognition and of emotion in the *Iliad*, 85 per cent of the occurrences of θυμός are in the emotional context.[59]

In order to make the discussion of verbs of emotion with θυμός less cumbersome, I have located the larger groups of passages under the heading of the relevant verb and without translations in the appendix, in the order of occurrence within the text. Several very small groups of passages will, however, be discussed within the text at the beginning of this section.

§39. Emotion: φιλέω: With the verb φιλέω, θυμός alone is used, as at I. 196 = 209:

---

[59] For purposes of simplicity only, the context of motivation, which will be discussed after the emotional context, was included in this count as emotional.

ἄμφω ὁμῶς θυμῷ φιλέουσά τε κηδομένη τε·

..... loving and caring for both alike in her θυμός;

At IX 343 and 482, the phrases ἐκ θυμοῦ φίλεον and ἐκ θυμοῦ φιλέων respectively are used, the θυμός being mentioned as the source of the feeling.

§40. Emotion: ἵμερος: The word ἵμερος "longing," does not fit neatly into the emotional context. It has overtones also of physical impulse, as will be seen from the following passages; and also it has a negative effect upon the ability to think rationally. At XI 89, hunger affects the φρένες:

σίτου τε γλυκεροῖο περὶ φρένας ἵμερος αἱρεῖ,

..... and the longing for sweet food seizes around his φρένες, ...

This passage is reminiscent of passages cited in §11, where θυμός experiences satiety.

At III 139–140, Helen experiences longing of a more emotional sort for her former life:

ὣς εἰποῦσα θεὰ γλυκὺν ἵμερον ἔμβαλε θυμῷ
ἀνδρός τε προτέρου καὶ ἄστεος ἠδὲ τοκήων·

Thus speaking, the goddess cast sweet longing upon her θυμός for her former husband and her city and her parents.

And at XIV 216–217, in the description of Aphrodite's girdle, the force of passion is said to impair the judgment:

ἔνθ' ἔνι μὲν φιλότης, ἐν δ' ἵμερος, ἐν δ' ὀαριστὺς
πάρφασις, ἥ τ' ἔκλεψε νόον πύκα περ φρονεόντων.

There is in it sexual passion and longing, and endearing seduction, which steals away the νόος of even those who use their φρένες in a careful way.

Φρήν/φρένες is thus the more frequent psychological entity, whether implied or expressed. This last passage suggests a connection with IX 550, where anger *swells* the νόος, and with the group of passages discussed in §35 on the ability of the gods to so charm men that their intellectual processes no longer function.[60] The emphasis in these cases tends to be, therefore, on the improper functioning of cognition.

§41. Emotion: ἔρος: Sexual desire is also expressed by ἔρος. At III 442, Paris urges Helen to join him in bed:

οὐ γάρ πώ ποτέ μ' ὧδέ γ' ἔρως φρένας ἀμφεκάλυψεν,

nor ever at any time has ἔρος thus surrounded my φρένες,

At XIV 294 a similar line occurs:

---

[60] See 35.

ὡς δ' ἴδεν, ὥς μιν ἔρως πυκινὰς φρένας ἀμφεκάλυψεν,

When he saw her, thus desire surrounded his close-knit φρένες,

But at XIV 315–316, θυμός is used:

οὐ γάρ πώ ποτέ μ' ὧδε θεᾶς ἔρος οὐδὲ γυναικὸς
θυμὸν ἐνὶ στήθεσσι περιπροχυθεὶς ἐδάμασσεν, ...

Nor has sexual desire for goddess or woman ever so subdued my θυμός in my chest, having been poured around (it), ...

Out of three passages, therefore, ἔρος affects the φρένες twice and the θυμός once. A brief summation of these ways of expressing love of both the emotional and the sexual variety finds θυμός used six times, φρένες four, and νόος once. Again, the focus of this group of passages is not on emotion but on the impairment of cognition.

§42. Emotion: ἰαίνω: The verb ἰαίνω occurs in two senses: the first and more literal one refers to the warming of water in a container over a fire, the second to a feeling of pleasure. The first sense occurs twice in the *Odyssey*:

viii	426	ἀμφὶ δέ οἱ πυρὶ χαλκὸν ἵηνατε, θέρμετε δ' ὕδωρ,
x	358–359	ἡ δὲ τετάρτη ὕδωρ ἐφόρει καὶ πῦρ ἀνέκαιε
		πολλὸν ὑπὸ τρίποδι μεγάλῳ· ἰαίνετο δ' ὕδωρ.

In the passages where ἰαίνω is used metaphorically, θυμός is generally the part of the person affected, φρένες occurring twice as the location:

XXIII	597	.... τοῖο δὲ θυμὸς
	598	ἰάνθη ὡς εἴ τε περὶ σταχύεσσιν ἐέρση
	599	ληΐου ἀλδήσκοντος, ὅτε φρίσσουσιν ἄρουραι·
	600	ὡς ἄρα σοί, Μενέλαε, μετὰ φρεσὶ θυμὸς ἰάνθη.
XXIV	119	
	147	δῶρα δ' Ἀχιλλῆϊ φερέμεν, τά κε θυμὸν ἰήνῃ.
	176	
	196	
xv	164	.... οἱ δὲ ἰδόντες
	165	γήθησαν, καὶ πᾶσιν ἐνὶ φρεσὶ θυμὸς ἰάνθη.
	379	..... οἷά τε θυμὸν ἀεὶ δμώεσσιν ἰαίνει.
H. Dem.	64	.... εἴ ποτε δή σευ
	65	ἢ ἔπει ἢ ἔργῳ κραδίην καὶ θυμὸν ἴηνα.
	434	ὣς τότε μὲν πρόπαν ἦμαρ ὁμόφρονα θυμὸν ἔχουσαι
	435	πολλὰ μάλ' ἀλλήλων κραδίην καὶ θυμὸν ἴαινον
	436	ἀμφαγαπαζόμεναι· ἀχέων δ' ἀπεπαύετο θυμός.

The φρένες are the location or the container of the θυμός, as was mentioned originally in connection with the return of consciousness after syncope in §5. Here, at xv 165, just as water must be warmed within a kind of vessel, θυμός is warmed in the φρένες. Κραδίη is used twice in the *Hymn to Demeter*, in combination with θυμός. In this context, θυμός, φρένες, and κράδιη can be considered functional synonyms; but only θυμός and κραδίη are directly affected by the action of the verb, whereas φρένες occurs in the dative as the location of the affected psychological entity.

§43. Emotion: ἀνδάνω: The verb ἀνδάνω occurs infrequently.[61] In the three relevant passages in the *Iliad*, all of which end with the same two-word phrase, it is used with θυμός; it is used once in the *Odyssey* with φρένες and βουλή in a passage which was discussed at §31.

§44. Emotion: γηθέω: Usage with γηθέω is more extensive and more varied, and should include the related noun γηθοσύνη and the related adjective γηθόσυνος. When any explanatory psychological term is used, θυμός and φρήν/φρένες occur more often in either the dative or the accusative case. Rare varieties of expression include ἦτορ and κῆρ in the adverbial accusative; μένος and βίη occur only as periphrases of the person concerned.

§45. Emotion: βούλομαι: Another word for wishing, βούλομαι, occurs only twice in the *Iliad* with θυμός and once in the *Hymn to Apollo*. The occurrence with a psychological term is so low that we can only note the preference for θυμός.

§46. Emotion: μενοινάω: The verb μενοινάω is used infrequently to express eagerness. The pertinent passages demonstrate that the terms θυμός and φρένες are used interchangeably, in the dative case.

§47. Emotion: τιτύσκομαι: The verb τιτύσκομαι "to take aim, be eager," occurs only with φρένες in the dative case.

§48. Emotion: ἴεμαι: The verb ἴεμαι "to be eager" occurs only four times, and only in the *Iliad*, with θυμός. As has been true in several other contexts, the incidence is too low by itself to encourage conclusions.

§49. Emotion: χαίρω: Far more evidence for the preference for θυμός in the emotional context is presented by usage with the verb χαίρω. Φρήν/φρένες, νόος, and κῆρ also occur as functional synonyms of θυμός but comparatively rarely. The list of passages in the appendix should speak for itself. Moreover, it is clear that the meter could have played only a minor role in restricting usage to θυμός since epic diction uses different forms of the verb at different positions in the line.

§50. Emotion: τέρπω: the verb τέρπω, usually in the middle voice, is used almost equally with θυμός (eleven times) or with φρήν/φρένες (eight times). Νόος occurs in only one passage. Usually the psychological term describes the location of the emotion rather than the affected part. At IX 185–189, however, atypically both φρήν and θυμός occur in the accusative as direct objects of the verb which is in the middle voice at 186 and in the active

---

[61] See the appendix.

voice at 189:

> Μυρμιδόνων δ'ἐπί τε κλισίας καὶ νῆας ἱκέσθην,
> τὸν δ'εὗρον <u>φρένα</u> <u>τερπόμενον</u> φόρμιγγι λιγείῃ,
> καλῇ δαιδαλέῃ, ἐπὶ δ' ἀργύρεον ζυγὸν ἦεν,
> τὴν ἄρετ' ἐξ ἐνάρων πόλιν Ἠετίωνος ὀλέσσας·
> τῇ ὅ γε <u>θυμὸν</u> <u>ἔτερπεν</u>, ἄειδε δ' ἄρα κλέα ἀνδρῶν.

They (two) came to the tents and ships of the Myrmidons, and they found him (Akhilleus) comforting his φρήν with a clear-voiced lyre, a lyre fairly wrought, and upon it was a silver bridge, the lyre which he had won from the spoils when he had destroyed Eetion's city; with this lyre he was delighting his θυμός and he was singing the fame of heroes.

Usage with τέρπω/τέρπομαι, therefore shows a very slight preference for θυμός as either the location or the affected part; and νόος is the only functional synonym.

§51. Emotion: ἔλπομαι: The verb ἔλπομαι is used far more often with θυμός than with φρήν/φρένες. Out of thirteen passages in the *Iliad*, it occurs with θυμός in all but one; and out of seven passages in the *Odyssey,* θυμός is used five times and φρένες twice. There are no other functional synonyms used.

§52. Emotion: ἐθέλω: There is again a decided preference for θυμός in combination with ἐθέλω. Φρένες occurs only once; and in this case, it is likely that it should actually be connected with the aorist active participle μερμηρίξας.[62] It must be significant that this verb occurs only with θυμός in both epics; and although six out of the ten passages in the *Odyssey* are formulae[63] for the satisfaction of hunger and thirst, the passages from the *Iliad* demonstrate sufficient variety that the meter cannot be claimed as a totally restrictive influence on choice of words. It is also significant that no other functional synonyms occur.

§53. Emotion: πείθω: In passages with πείθω, there is more equal distribution between use of θυμός and φρήν/φρένες as the parts affected.[64] But again, there are real differences between usage in the *Iliad* and that in the *Odyssey*. Typically, the passages in the *Odyssey* demonstrate greater uniformity; and only one makes use of φρένες. In the *Iliad,* however, the distribution is equal between the two functional synonyms; and there is far greater variety of expression.

---

[62] Φρήν/φρένες occurs with μερμηρίζειν at II 3, V 671, VIII 169; i 427 x 50, 151, 438, xi 204, xvi 73, xx 10, 38, 41, 93, xxii 333, xxiv 128, 235.

[63] I do not wish to enter into a discussion of what does or does not constitute a formula or a formulaic line. It should be self-evident here that five out of the six lines from the *Odyssey* are identical, and that the sixth line describing satiety varies only slightly. What is perhaps far more interesting is the fact that usage in the *Iliad* is very fluid in contrast to usage in the *Odyssey*.

[64] With reservations and partly for convenience, I have classified πείθω as emotional; happily this point of view is supported overtly by at least one passage, i.e. xxiii 230.

§54. Emotion: endurance: Endurance is expressed in several different ways, by the verbs ἀνέχω, τολμάω and τλάω; and by the adjectives τλήμων and τλητός. With the exception of one passage each from the *Iliad* and from the *Odyssey* where φρένες is used in the dative, θυμός is the part involved in the act of enduring.[65] Judging from the fact that θυμός is modified by the relevant adjectives, it was considered by Homeric diction the faculty capable of enduring; and also judging from the context of these passages, the endurance is emotional in nature. Moreover, φρένες occurs only in the dative plural, thus being relegated to the location of this activity. It would seem here, then, that θυμός was felt to be an aspect of the emotional nature of the individual. And interestingly enough, the location of θυμός when specified is always in the φρένες or the στήθεα, the most common alternative expression of location. Granted that passages specifying location number only four out of eighteen; this fact will appear more significant when it is compared later with the location of θυμός in diction describing the absence of emotional endurance.

Again it should be noticed that the larger part of examples from the *Odyssey* are repetitive, whereas the *Iliad* never repeats the expression of this state in identical lines or phrases: nine out of ten times in the *Odyssey*, the phrase τετληότι θυμῷ occurs at the end of the line.

§55. Emotion: χόλος, etc.: Descriptions of anger are frequent in early Greek epic, θυμός being found with χολόω, χόλος, and χώομαι. In §33, it was mentioned that χόλος, in Homeric diction, causes the νόος to swell. In several passages from the *Iliad*, χόλος falls upon the θυμός, a curious and graphic way of describing the entrance of a new substance into the hitherto unperturbed human interior. Out of 15 passages from the *Iliad*, θυμός is used in twelve and φρένες in two. Out of seven in the *Odyssey*, φρήν and θυμός each occur in one; κηρόθι occurs in five within the phrase κηρόθι μᾶλλον at the end of the line, preceded by some form of the verbs χολόω or χώομαι. Out of three occurrences in Hesiod, φρένες, θυμός and ἦτορ each occur once. In the *Hymn to Demeter*, θυμός is used. There is thus a definite preference for θυμός in this context, a preference to be only slightly underestimated in relation to the formula κηρόθι μᾶλλον from the *Odyssey*.

§56. Emotion: θύω, μαίνομαι, etc.: There are a few unusual ways of describing anger. At *Iliad* I 342, the phrase ὀλοιῇσι φρεσὶ θύει is used. At VIII 413, the ἦτορ is located in the φρένες: . . . . . τί σφῶιν ἐνὶ φρεσὶ μαίνεται ἦτορ. At *Iliad* XIV 191, the expression used is κοτεσσαμένη τό γε θυμῷ. At *Theogony* 617-618, yet another verb is used with θυμός:

Ὀβριάρεῳ δ' ὡς πρῶτα πατὴρ ὠδύσσατο θυμῷ

---

[65] See XVIII 430, xix 347.

Κόττῳ τ' ἠδὲ Γύγῃ, ...

And when their father was first angry in his θυμός at Obriareus and Kottos and Gyges . . . .

The incidence of these unusual expressions is too insignificant to encourage drawing conclusions.

§57. Emotion: grief: In the expression of grief, there is again a wide variety and θυμός/φρήν/φρένες/κῆρ/κραδίη/ἦτορ function as synonyms. However, the passages themselves show a decided preference for θυμός as the subject or object of the verb, or as the location or indirect object of the emotion. Φρένες, which in any case is preferred as the location, occurs less than half as often as θυμός. The verbs and nouns included in this group are as follows: ἀχεύω, ἄχνυμαι, ἀκαχίζω, κήδω, ὀδύρομαι, ὀλοφύρομαι, στεναχίζω, συνέχω, φθίω, and then ἄλγος, ἄχος, κῆδος, μελέδημα, πένθος, and ὀδύνη. It will again be noticed in the passages cited in the appendix that repetition of formulae accounts for a larger number of passages from the *Odyssey* than from the *Iliad*.

§58. Emotion: κατέδω, δάκνω: Epic diction depicts the θυμός, and less often the φρένες, as being bitten or devoured in difficult situations. For example, at VI 200–202, Bellerophon's isolation is described:

ἀλλ' ὅτε δὴ καὶ κεῖνος ἀπήχθετο πᾶσι θεοῖσιν,
ἤτοι ὁ κὰπ πεδίον τὸ Ἀλήϊον οἶος ἀλᾶτο,
ὃν θυμὸν κατέδων, πάτον ἀνθρώπων ἀλεείνων·

But when indeed he was hated by all the gods, then he wandered alone over the Aleian plain, devouring his own θυμός, shunning the path of men;

A similar expression occurs at ix 75 and x 143:

κείμεθ' ὁμοῦ καμάτῳ τε καὶ ἄλγεσι θυμὸν ἔδοντες.

We lay together eating our θυμός with weariness and cares.

At V 493, the φρένες are affected:

Ὣς φάτο Σαρπηδών, δάκε δὲ φρένας Ἕκτορι μῦθος·

Sarpedon spoke thus, and his speech bit the φρένες of Hektor.

And at viii 185, Euryalos' challenge to Odysseus is a biting one, θυμοδακής γὰρ μῦθος.

§59. Emotion: Other unusual expressions for grief: There are four other metaphorical expressions used to describe grief, all suggesting a physical affect upon the θυμός/φρήν/φρένες. At XVII 564 (and see also XX 425), the effect of Patroklos' death upon others is described thus:

. . . . μάλα γάρ με θανὼν ἐσεμάσσατο θυμόν.

. . . . for in dying he touched my θυμός.

At V 748, the same verbal root is used with a different prefix:[66]

"Ἥρη δὲ μάστιγι θοῶς ἐπεμαίετο ἄρα ἵππους·

Hera lashed the horses swiftly with a whip; .....

It would seem, therefore, that behind the metaphorical expression in the first passage cited here, there is a literal sense implying again that the θυμός has a substantial nature.

Intensity of emotion is also conveyed by the use of the verb ἀμύσσω with θυμός. At XIX 284–285, ἀμύσσω is used of the laceration of the breast in mourning:

ἀμφ' αὐτῷ χυμένη λίγ' ἐκώκυε, χερσὶ δ' ἄμυσσε
στήθεά τ' ἠδ' ἀπαλὴν δειρὴν ἰδὲ καλὰ πρόσωπα.

..... pouring herself about him, she cried shrilly, and she tore her breast with her hands, and her soft neck and fair face.

At I 243–244, Akhilleus predicts to Agamemnon how he will feel if the leader of the Greeks should persist in his current course of action:

.... σὺ δ' ἔνδοθι θυμὸν ἀμύξεις
χωόμενος ὅ τ' ἄριστον Ἀχαιῶν οὐδὲν ἔτεισας.

.... but you will tear the θυμός within, angered that you have not honored the best of the Achaians.

The θυμός will be self-mutilated, as though in mourning for the irrevocable death of a beloved friend.

§60. Grief: summary: In a brief summary of the category of grief, therefore, θυμός, φρήν/φρένες, κῆρ, κραδίη and ἦτορ are functional synonyms, and θυμός occurs 2 ½ times more often than the next most frequently-used term, φρένες. Also, in the metaphorical expressions used to describe the effect of grief upon the individual, θυμός is the preferred word. In passages with κατέδω δάκνω, ἐσμάιομαι, and ἀμύσσω, epic diction suggests that the θυμός experiences physical harm from grief.

§61. Emotion: misc.: There are several minor categories within the context of emotion which occur only with θυμός; the total of these passages is too slight to offer conclusive evidence, but they confirm the importance of θυμός in this context. These are passages on blame or criticism with the verbs νεμεσάω and νεμεσίζομαι and the noun ἐνίπη at XIV 104–105, XVI 544, and ii 138; on the act of prayer, as at XXIII 768–769; on exultation with the verbs μεγαλίζομαι at X 69 and βλεμεαίνω at XVII 22; on the act of threatening with the verb ἀπειλέω at XV 212; and finally on rage, ἀλύσσω, in the θυμός of dogs at XXII 70.

---

[66] Chantraine, 658–659.

§62. Emotion: αἰδώς: Equally important for the understanding of θυμός in epic diction are descriptions of the restraint of emotion, for they depict an opposite movement as it were. In this category, θυμός/φρήν/φρένες are used as functional synonyms, but θυμός is the preferred expression. First, restraint exercised on an individual through a sense of shame is felt in the φρένες at X 237-238:

μηδὲ σύ γ' αἰδόμενος σῇσι φρεσὶ τὸν μὲν ἀρείω
καλλείπειν, σὺ δὲ χεῖρον' ὀπάσσεαι αἰδοῖ εἴκων,

Do not, even though you feel shame in your φρένες leave behind the better man, and take the worse in yielding to shame, ...

And at XV 561/661:

ὦ φίλοι, ἀνέρες ἔστε, καὶ αἰδῶ θέσθ' ἐνὶ θυμῷ,

O friends, be men, and put shame in your θυμός . . . . .

Here θυμός and φρένες are functional synonyms.

§63. Emotion: σέβας, σεβάζομαι: σέβας/σεβάζομαι are used to describe restraint, but only in relation to the θυμός. At VI 166-167, King Proitos holds back from killing Bellerophon, although his wife Anteia claimed an attempt at seduction:

ὣς φάτο, τὸν δὲ ἄνακτα χόλος λάβεν οἷον ἄκουσε·
κτεῖναι μέν ῥ ἀλέεινε, σεβάσσατο γὰρ τό γε θυμῷ,

Thus she spoke, and anger seized the lord at what he heard; he shrank from killing him, and restrained it (the murderous impulse) in his θυμός, ...

At VI 417, Akhilleus is said to have restrained himself from stripping Eetion of his armor:

οὐδέ μιν ἐξενάριζε, σεβάσσατο γὰρ τό γε θυμῷ, ...

but he did not strip him, for he held back in his θυμός from that . . . . .

At XVIII 178-179, Iris urges Akhilleus to return to battle:

ἀλλ' ἄνα, μηδ' ἔτι κεῖσο· σέβας δέ σε θυμὸν ἱκέσθω . . . . .

But up, do not stay lying around; let restraint come to your θυμός (restraint from allowing Patroklos to become spoil for the Trojan dogs) . . . . .

For Akhilleus, return to battle would mark the end of his uncontrolled wrath.

§64. Emotion: ἐρητύω: Restraint is also expressed with the verb ἐρητύω with which θυμός, θυμός ἐνὶ φρεσί, and κραδίη are used. At IX 635, a man who has received payment for the killing of a kinsman or a child and who forbears from taking vengeance restrains himself, in contrast to Akhilleus, who refuses to yield to the entreaties of the Greeks:

> τοῦ δέ τ' ἐρητύεται κραδίη καὶ θυμὸς ἀγήνωρ
>
> ..... and this man's heart and manly θυμός are restrained, ...

It should be remembered that at XXII 357, Akhilleus' heart is described as σιδήρεος by Hektor, and that here at IX 636 it is called κακός and ἄλληκτος.

But ἐρητύω expresses not mere restraint: in two passages it is used to describe the containment of the θυμός within the φρένες. This concept was mentioned in 5; also, there are numerous descriptions of emotion which locate the θυμός within the φρένες. Here the result of lack of containment is made explicit. At IX 458–459, Phoinix describes his final quarrel with his father, his refusal to remain restrained and confined:

> ἔνθ' ἐμοὶ οὐκέτι πάμπαν ἐρητύετ' ἐν φρεσὶ θυμός
> πατρὸς χωομένοιο κατὰ μέγαρα στρωφᾶσθαι.
>
> Then no longer could the θυμός be confined entirely in my φρένες to frequent the house, since my father was in a state of rage.

Once his θυμός passed the bounds of his φρένες, he himself escaped from his father's house. Emotional restraint again is synonymous with restraint in action, restraint in the sense of acting in the way that is expected of one. The same equation between the physical and the emotional levels is made in the description of the coward at XIII 279–283:

> τοῦ μὲν γάρ τε κακοῦ τρέπεται χρὼς ἄλλυδις ἄλλη,
> οὐδέ οἱ ἀτρέμας ἧσθαι ἐρητύετ' ἐν φρεσὶ θυμός,
> ἀλλὰ μετοκλάζει καὶ ἐπ' ἀμφοτέρους πόδας ἵζει,
> ἐν δέ τέ οἱ κραδίη μεγάλα στέρνοισι πατάσσει
> κῆρας ὀϊομένῳ, πάταγος δέ τε γίγνετ' ὀδόντων·
>
> for the color (skin) of the coward changes from one to another, nor is his θυμός contained to rest untrembling in his φρένες, but he shifts his weight from thigh to thigh, and from foot to foot; and within his chest his heart pounds greatly as he thinks of death, and there arises a chattering of the teeth.

Again, the lack of emotional restraint is the result of the θυμός having parted company with the φρένες, as it were. This basic physiological fact gives rise to an extreme emotional condition, the symptoms of which are physical reactions such as pallor and trembling.

§65. Emotion: δαμάζω: In a limited number of passages, the verb δαμάζω expresses subjugation of one impulse to another, always in the sense of subduing the θυμός. In one case, the context is the power of eroticism over the rest of the person, in the seduction of Zeus by Hera, specifically at XIV 315–316:

> οὐ γάρ ποτέ μ' ὧδε θεᾶς ἔρος οὐδὲ γυναικὸς
> θυμὸν ἐνὶ στήθεσσι περιπροχυθεὶς ἐδάμασσεν, ...

> Never had desire for goddess or woman, pouring around the θυμός in my chest, so subdued me . . . . .

The yielding of Zeus is thus not so different from Akhilleus' eventual yielding to the entreaties of the Greeks at XVIII 112–113:

ἀλλὰ τὰ μὲν προτετύχθαι ἐάσομεν ἀχνύμενοί περ,
θυμὸν ἐνὶ στήθεσσι φίλον δαμάσαντες ἀνάγκῃ·

> but although grieved, we shall let these things go as having been done in the past, subduing by necessity the dear θυμός in the breast.

It is in exactly these terms that Phoinix entreats him at IX 496–498 to give up his intransigence:

ἀλλ', Ἀχιλεῦ, δάμασον θυμὸν μέγαν· οὐδέ τί σε χρὴ
νηλεὲς ἦτορ ἔχειν· στρεπτοὶ δὲ καὶ θεοὶ αὐτοί,
τῶν περ καὶ μείζων ἀρετὴ τιμή τε βίη τε.

> But Akhilleus, tame your great θυμός; it is in no way necessary that you have a pitiless heart; even the gods themselves are capable of being turned, they whose excellence and honor and might are greater.

In every case, the location of θυμός is given as the chest or the φρένες. At v 468 and xi 562, the θυμός is subdued but not expressly located.

§66. *Emotion: summary*: In an overview of the context of emotions, it can be seen that θυμός plays a more important role than any of its other functional synonyms. Κῆρ/κραδίη/ἦτορ are rare and occur almost always in frequently-used formulaic lines; and φρήν/φρένες occurs more frequently as the location of the emotion or of θυμός itself. The location of θυμός within or outside of the φρήν/φρένες is, in fact, shown by epic diction to be vital to the current state of the θυμός and hence of the individual. The physical state of θυμός also plays a role in this context, in that grief is seen to injure it. And in the process of restraining the intense emotions in which θυμός is seen to play a role, this psychological entity is kept within the φρένες; conversely, when feelings become so intense that behavior itself can no longer be contained, the θυμός is seen as having passed the bounds of the φρένες. Early Greek poetry offers examples of different stages of semantic specialization; and particularly in the context of emotions, for the reasons just cited, θυμός seems to be in the process of becoming no longer the neutral bearer of emotions but emotion itself.

§67. *Inner debate*: As was mentioned at the beginning of this chapter, it would not be strictly in keeping with Homeric diction itself to classify every passage in which θυμός occurs as pertaining to death/loss of consciousness, cognition, or emotion. Some of the passages already cited are, in fact, either anomalous or more complex. But there are two groups of passages which have been put under separate headings because they formed such distinct groupings: the first of these describes the condition of inner debate or conflict, and the second that of inner motivation. The first group, passages describing inner debate, are identified by the presence of the verbs ὁρμαίνω, μερμηρίζω, and διαλέγομαι. In some passages, the inner conflict is emphasized by the adverbs δίχα, διχθά, and διάνδιχα; and in almost all cases, the inner elements mentioned are θυμός and φρήν, particularly in the phrase κατὰ φρένα καὶ κατὰ θυμόν.

§68. Inner debate: ὁρμαίνω: The verb ὁρμαίνω occurs fourteen times in the Homeric poems with the phrase κατὰ φρένα καὶ κατὰ θυμόν.[67] But perhaps the ideal passage is to be found at XI 401–411 in the description of Odysseus' inner state when he finds himself isolated from his fighting companions on the battle field:

Οἰώθη δ' Ὀδυσεὺς δουρικλυτός, οὐδέ τις αὐτῷ
Ἀργείων παρέμεινεν, ἐπεὶ φόβος ἔλλαβε πάντας·
ὀχθήσας δ' ἄρα εἶπε πρὸς ὃν μεγαλήτορα θυμόν·
"ὤμοι ἐγώ, τί πάθω; μέγα μὲν κακὸν αἴ κε φέβωμαι
πληθὺν ταρβήσας· τὸ δὲ ρίγιον αἴ κεν ἁλώω
μοῦνος· τοὺς δ' ἄλλους Δαναοὺς ἐφόβησε Κρονίων.
ἀλλὰ τίη μοι ταῦτα φίλος διελέξατο θυμός;
οἶδα γὰρ ὅττι κακοὶ μὲν ἀποίχονται πολέμοιο,
ὃς δέ κ' ἀριστεύῃσι μάχῃ ἔνι, τὸν δὲ μάλα χρεώ
ἑστάμεναι κρατερῶς, ἤ τ' ἔβλητ' ἤ τ' ἔβαλ' ἄλλον."
ἧος ὁ ταῦθ' ὥρμαινε κατὰ φρένα καὶ κατὰ θυμόν,

Odysseus reknowned for the spear was left alone, nor did any one of the Argives remain beside him, since panic had seized them all; grieving, he spoke to his great-hearted θυμός: "O woe is me, what am I to endure? It is a great act of cowardice if I should take flight, terrified by the numbers of men; but it will be worse if I am taken alone; the son of Kronos put the other Danaans to flight. But why has my dear θυμός discussed these things in me? I know that cowards leave the battle, but he who excels in battle must stand his ground strongly, whether he is hit or hits another." And while he was debating these things in his φρήν and in his θυμός, ...

Odysseus is terrified of being overcome by the Trojans, but his training to be brave in battle and not to flee causes the inner conflict; for how he *should* behave is opposed to how he would *like* to behave. Both emotion and cognition play important roles here and in the other passages and are signalled by the repeated phrase κατὰ φρένα καὶ κατὰ θυμόν. In this entire group of passages, κραδίη occurs only once as the functional synonym of θυμός/φρήν/φρένες.

§69. Inner debate: ὁρμαίνω: At XIV 16–24, the state of being in conflict is again described by the verb ὁρμαίνω, the participle δαϊζόμενος, and the

---

[67] XI 411, XVII 106, XVIII 15, iv 120, v 365 and 424 are identical. vi 118 begins slightly differently.

adverb διχθάδια. The weather simile, as will be shown in Chapter IV, is extremely important to the understanding of the associations of θυμός, which occurs here alone:

ὡς δ' ὅτε πορφύρῃ πέλαγος μέγα κύματι κωφῷ,
ὀσσόμενον λιγέων ἀνέμων λαιψηρὰ κέλευθα
αὔτως, οὐδ' ἄρα τε προκυλίνδεται οὐδετέρωσε,
πρίν τινα κεκριμένον καταβήμεναι ἐκ Διὸς οὖρον,
ὣς ὁ γέρων ὥρμαινε δαϊζόμενος κατὰ θυμὸν
διχθάδι', ἢ μεθ' ὅμιλον ἴοι Δαναῶν ταχυπώλων,
ἦε μετ' Ἀτρεΐδην Ἀγαμέμνονα, ποιμένα λαῶν.
ὧδε δέ οἱ φρονέοντι δοάσσατο κέρδιον εἶναι,
βῆναι ἐπ' Ἀτρεΐδην..........

Just as when the great sea heaves with a ground-swell, awaiting in the same place the rushing paths of the shrill winds, and does not roll forward on either side, until a decisive wind comes down from Zeus, thus the old man debated, divided two ways in his θυμός, whether he should go into the throng of the Danaans of the swift horses, or go for Atreides Agamemnon, shepherd of the people. And thus it seemed better to him as he pondered to go to Atreides.

Nestor is in conflict how to act; his θυμός heaves, as it were, with the tension of indecision, until the process of φρονέω, acting like the decisive wind from Zeus, pushes him in a definite direction

§70. Inner debate: μερμηρίζω: Inner debate or conflict is also described by the verb μερμηρίζω, with θυμός/φρήν/φρένες/ἦτορ as the inner faculties affected. Out of all seventeen passages in which μερμηρίζω occurs with an inner faculty, ἦτορ is found only once and is located in the chest. The remaining three passages from the *Iliad* use φρήν once by itself and twice in parallel construction with θυμός. In the *Odyssey*, θυμός occurs once alone, once in conjunction with the verb φράσσω, once with the verb δοκέω but in the same line with μερμηρίζω; φρένες occurs four times by itself in the dative case; and both θυμός and φρήν/φρένες occur together six times, in three cases in the phrase κατὰ φρένα καὶ κατὰ θυμόν and twice in the phrase θυμὸς ἐνὶ φρεσί. The passages are to be found in the appendix.

§71. Inner debate: διαλέγομαι: A third way of describing inner debate appears in the following line, which is repeated five times in the *Iliad*:[68]

ἀλλὰ τίη μοι ταῦτα φίλος διελέξατο θυμός;

But why has my dear θυμός discussed these things with me?

Each of these lines occurs in a context of intense emotion. As with passages in which θυμός is used with the verb μερμηρίζω, there is a strong sense of inner division. But this category of passages relies for its effect on the metaphor of inner dialogue; and the inner division is marked only by the

---

[68] XI 407, XVII 97, XXI 562, XXII 122, 385.

prefix δια-.

§72. Inner debate: summary: In this context, therefore, θυμός/φρήν/φρένες/ ἦτορ are used as functional synonyms, with a definite preference for the first three. In five out of the fifteen passages including μερμηρίζω, θυμός and φρήν occur in parallel construction; in all but two of the rest, θυμός/ φρήν/φρένες are to be found. In passages with ὁρμαίνω, θυμός/φρήν in parallel construction occurs seven out of a total of fourteen times, five of those being in a repeated formulaic line. Κραδίη occurs only once as a functional synonym, and the remaining passages use θυμός/φρήν/ φρένες. Only in passages with διαλέγομαι is θυμός used exclusively.

§73. Motivation: In the last context to be discussed, that of motivation, it is particularly clear that the passages do not belong solely in any other context. They are emotionally neutral and at the same time do not have to do specifically with cognition. The metaphor common to all of them is that of speech, the command given to the inner man to act in a certain way. Θυμός/ κραδίη/μένος function as synonyms in this group of passages, with φρένες appearing only once as the location of the action.

Out of eighteen occurrences in the *Iliad* with the inner faculty expressed, θυμός appears sixteen times alone (two of these times located in the στήθεα), once in parallel construction with μένος, and only once in the dative case. Out of ten passages in the *Odyssey*, ἦτορ is the subject of the verb only once. In all other passages, θυμός is the subject of the verb, occuring only once in combination with κραδίη.

§74. Motivation, cont.: Beyond the statistics, which show almost exclusive use of θυμός, it is important to understand that this phrasing of the inner command, the call to action coming from within, is not an expression of impulse. In all cases, the action bidden is appropriate to the circumstances. To cite an example, at VI 441–449 the action is well-considered, the result of training, and goes counter to other strong impulses. And at times, the personal urging comes simultaneously with the urging of a god, as at IX 702–703 and in XXIV, where Priam and Akhilleus are motivated both by personal wish and by divine requirements. Even in the *Odyssey,* where the phrase "my θυμός bids me" is reduced almost to the level of "I want", the actions thus motivated are appropriate to the circumstances.

§75. Motivation: ὀτρύνω The verb ὀτρύνω is also used to indicate inner motivation. There is one formulaic line, ὣς εἰπὼν ὄτρυνε μένος καὶ θυμὸν ἑκάστου, which is used ten times in the *Iliad* and only once in the *Odyssey*. In one other case, μένος and θυμός occur in parallel construction as the direct object of the verb. In three cases, κραδίη and θυμός occur as subjects of the verb. Μένος and θυμός each occur only once by themselves as the subject of the verb. Φρήν/φρένες do not appear at all; on the contrary, θυμός is present in every case except one.

§76. Motivation: ἀνίημι : ἀνίημι is used eleven times in the *Iliad* with θυμός and one of those times with μένος also. This usage does not occur at all in the *Odyssey*.

§77. Motivation: κελεύω, κέλομαι: κελεύω and κέλομαι are used also with θυμός to describe inner motivation. The most frequently-occuring line in this category is:

ὄφρ' εἴπω τά με θυμὸς ἐνὶ στήθεσσι κελεύει.

..... so that I may say what the θυμός in my breast bids me.

Κραδίη occurs as the subject of the verb in parallel construction with θυμός in the phrase κραδίη θυμός τε κελεύει. With κέλομαι, θυμός is the subject and occurs three times in the phrase κέλεται δέ με θυμός and only once as κέλεται δέ ἑ θυμὸς ἀγήνωρ. Here θυμός has no functional synonyms.

§78. Motivation: ἐφορμάομαι, ἐποτρύνω, ἀνώγω, ἐπισσεύω: There are in this context several verbs which do not occur frequently but which are particularly important for a thorough understanding of the associations of θυμός. The first of these, ἐφορμάομαι, is used only with θυμός. Ἐποτρύνω occurs twice in parallel construction with ἀνώγω and another three times by itself. Θυμός and μένος are functional synonyms in this group of passages, φρένες occuring only in the dative as the location of μένος. *Odyssey* ix 138–139 will be discussed later; but it should be noticed here that this passage shows associations with weather, a theme which is present in *Iliad* XIV 16–24 as mentioned in §69. Furthermore, the language is reminiscent of *Iliad* V 697–698, where Boreas returns the θυμός to Sarpedon. The verb ἐπισσεύω occurs with θυμός alone, and significantly, since it also is used of setting in motion and has associations with winds and weather.

§79. Motivation: ὀρίνω: Finally, the verb ὀρίνω is used with θυμός to describe inner motivation, nineteen times in the *Iliad* and eleven times in the *Odyssey*. Θυμός is always either the subject of the passive verb or the object of the active verb. Ἦτορ and κῆρ occur respectively twice and once as functional synonyms of θυμός; and the phrases ἐνὶ στήθεσσι and ἐνὶ φρεσί occur eight times and once respectively to indicate the location of the activity. Generally, a speech, an important event, or a divine agent cause the θυμός/ἦτορ/κῆρ to be aroused in these terms. In this group of passages, θυμός is decidely the dominant element.

§80. Motivation: ὀρίνω, cont.: The fact that the verb ὀρίνω is not a simple equivalent for the arousing of emotion becomes clearer upon examining its use in descriptions of weather. The particular association is that with storm winds, as can be seen from the following passages, II 292–294, IX 4–7, XI 296–298, and vii 271–274:

AN ANALYSIS OF THE USAGE OF ΘΥΜΟΣ IN EARLY GREEK EPIC   49

καὶ γάρ τίς θ' ἕνα μῆνα μένων ἀπὸ ἧς ἀλόχοιο
ἀσχαλάᾳ σὺν νηὶ πολυζύγῳ, ὅν περ ἄελλαι
χειμέριαι εἰλέωσιν ὀρινομένη τε θάλασσα·

For anyone who stays away from his wife for one month chafes in the many-benched ship, him whom the wintry blasts hold back, and the stirred-up sea.

ὡς δ' ἄνεμοι δύο πόντον ὀρίνετον ἰχθυόεντα,
Βορέης καὶ Ζέφυρος, τώ τε Θρήκηθεν ἄητον,
ἐλθόντ' ἐξαπίνης· ἄμυδις δέ τε κῦμα κελαινὸν
κορθύεται, πολλὸν δὲ παρὲξ ἅλα φῦκος ἔχευεν·

Thus two winds stir up the fishy sea, Boreas and Zephyr, who blow down from Thrace, coming all of a sudden; and the dark water is heaped up in a mass, and far across the salt water it has scattered the seaweed;

αὐτὸς δ' ἐν πρώτοισι μέγα φρονέων ἐβεβήκει,
ἐν δ' ἔπεσ' ὑσμίνῃ ὑπεραέϊ ἶσος ἀέλλῃ,
ἥ τε καθαλλομένη ἰοειδέα πόντον ὀρίνει.

And he himself, thinking great thoughts, went into the front ranks, and he fell upon the fray like a blast of wind from on high which, rushing down, stirs up the dark sea.

..... τήν μοι ἐπῶρσε Ποσειδάων ἐνοσίχθων,
ὅς μοι ἐφορμήσας ἀνέμους κατέδησε κελεύθου,
  ρινεν δὲ θάλασσαν ἀθέσφατον, οὐδέ τε κῦμα
εἴα ἐπὶ σχεδίης ἁδινὰ στενάχοντα φέρεσθαι.

(grief) which Poseidon the earth-shaker stirred up for me, he who in having roused the winds blew me off course, and he stirred up an unspeakable sea, and the swell did not let me be carried on the raft, as I groaned unceasingly.

§81. Motivation: summary: Θυμός is the essential word in the context of motivation. It appears in conjunction with ὀτρύνω and with μένος as its functional synonym more frequently than any other psychological term. Only in a very small number of cases do ἦτορ/κῆρ/κραδίη replace it. In general, this context is characterized by intensity, but not necessarily by violence. Often the motivating force is a divine agent, and the inner conflict in the individual is likened in several instances, as we have seen, to a violent storm at sea. The verbs ὀρίνω and ἐπισσεύομαι especially have close associations with storms and winds; and in these two groups of passages, θυμός is respectively the dominant and the unique psychological term used.

§82. Summary: Examination of the use of θυμός in all five contexts has yielded the following results:

1. Loss of consciousness/death: θυμός/μένος/ψυχή function as synonyms at the moment of loss of consciousness/death. At revival, only θυμός can return to the individual. On the other hand, only the ψυχή can go to the underworld, for the θυμός does not survive death. Θυμός also demonstrates associations with winds in this context, and is located in the φρήν during the state of consciousness. Θυμός is affected by the life of the body; but its substance is visualized by epic diction as being different from that of the φρένες. The place of the θυμός is in the φρήν/φρένες during consciousness; and it is conceived of as flexible in its proper state, whereas the φρένες are properly "close-knit".

2. Intellect/cognition: the apparent synonymity among θυμός, νόος, and φρήν/φρένες is rather an indissoluble connection between the two functions of thinking and feeling. Again in this context, the θυμός must be in the φρένες in order to function properly. It can also be surmised that the presence of θυμός in some passages of a primarily cognitive nature suggests an admixture in the intellectual function of feeling.

3. Emotion: θυμός plays the most important role in this context of any of its functional synonyms. Its functional synonyms ἦτορ/κῆρ/κραδίη occur infrequently, and φρήν/φρένες usually appears as the location rather than the psychological element directly affected. The fact that θυμός is the constant factor in passages describing a large number of emotions suggests that it itself is the neutral bearer of emotion.

4. Inner debate/conflict: θυμός/φρήν/φρένες/ἦτορ function as synonyms, with preference for the first three in parallel construction. Since these passages describe the inner conflict caused by the need to make a choice between two alternative courses of action, it seems reasonable to suppose that epic diction remains true to the inner complexity by including both intellectual and emotional factors.

5. Motivation: θυμός/μένος/ἦτορ/κῆρ/κραδίη are functional synonyms, but θυμός is by far the most frequently used. Location, when mentioned, is usually ἐνὶ στήθεσσι and rarely ἐνὶ φρεσί. This context is characterized by intensity, which is often amplified by the presence of a divine agent. This group of passages also demonstrates a very significant association with winds and storms on the part of verbs used with θυμός to describe inner motivation.

§83. Summary, cont.: It has been seen, therefore, that θυμός plays a definite role in each context. Its function in the inner life of the individual is bound up with its relationship to the φρήν/φρένες, not strictly as a synonym, for this relationship seems to be rather that of contained to container. When the θυμός is not contained in the φρήν/φρένες, the intellectual function is impaired and the emotions become uncontrollable. Hence no doubt the later semantic developments of θυμός which came to be thought of as violent emotion *per se*. And no doubt also, this later development depends to a certain extent on the fact that inner turmoil when pictured in terms of the θυμός is compared to violent storms and winds on the water.

CHAPTER FOUR

ΘΥΜΟΣ EXAMINED FURTHER: CONNECTIONS WITH THE WINDS

In the summary at the end of the last chapter, it was shown that θυμός in Homeric diction follows certain patterns which become apparent only after an examination of all the contexts in which it occurs. Though the analysis untangles much of the confusion surrounding this word, yet one more step needs to be taken; for underlying its importance in the inner psychology/physiology of the human organism are other less obvious though closely related associations which have been touched on but not yet fully discussed.

The etymology of θυμός is not fully solved, more because of the extent of its application than because of available evidence. Plato connected θυμός with the verb θύω, a relationship which can be fully accepted in light of its associations with the winds. Furthermore, the relationship to *fumus* as well as the semantic divergence from it will be understandable.[1] The connection of the noun ψυχή to the verb ψύχω having been found acceptable, there will be little difficulty in going one step further. For θυμός the missing link is to be found in the context of winds and storms, where θύειν describes the movement of storm winds, and to which winds the movement of θυμός within the individual in conflict is compared.[2]

In the examination of the characteristics exhibited by θυμός in the different contexts, it was found that epic diction endows the word with certain definite characteristics which are not applied to other psychic entities. First, and perhaps most noticeably, θυμός has a consistent relationship with φρήν/φρένες which is often expressed overtly. For instance, Andromakhe's revival is dependant upon the return of the θυμός to the φρήν.[3] In the discussion of the relative attributes of θυμός and φρήν/φρένες,[4] it was seen that the latter are appropriately of a close-knit texture and the former appropriately airy and flexible. Akhilleus' iron θυμός is the tragic flaw upon which the plot of the entire *Iliad* depends: even the gods have a θυμός which can be turned. Can this intransigence even be described as the temporary absence of intelligence, due to the failure of the θυμός to function as it should? In §19, the thematic connection between breath and intelligence

---

[1] Chapter 3, 69 ff.
[2] Chapter 3, 5, 20.
[3] Chapter 3, 14–17.
[4] Chapter 3, 66.

was made in relation to xxi 343=355, where Penelope puts the μῦθος πεπνυμένος of her son into her θυμός. It is true that φρήν/φρένες is found more frequently in the intellectual context than is θυμός; but for the intellect to function rightly, these two psychic entities must be in the proper relationship to each other. The relationship of θυμός to φρήν/φρένες is that of content to container. It is in the light of this relationship that we can better appreciate why θυμός must be flexible and φρήν/φρένες close-knit, and why also the physical impairment of φρήν/φρένες results in the lack of intelligence.[5]

Θυμός dominates the emotional context, although φρήν/φρένες occurs often and other functional synonyms much less often. The concept of containment is particularly important here: the escape of θυμός in extreme action on the part of the individual affected.[6] The behavior of Phoinix as a young man and that of the classic coward are perhaps the two most striking examples of "uncontained" individuals, aside from Akhilleus. It must be admitted that the volume of evidence for this concept is not overwhelming in relation to the total number of passages. However, the sequence of events is repeated on the cosmic level. We need only think of the beginning of *Odyssey* x, where Odysseus is granted fair passage when all the winds but one are safely bagged; when they are released, he is blown off course.[7] Moreover, θυμός has a number of associations with winds and storms.

Not only is the overt connection made in Homeric diction between the violence of the winds on the cosmic level and the forceful inner movement of the θυμός on the individual level; but there are coincidences in vocabulary with words which are not otherwise frequently used. These words are ἄημι, ἄητος, θύω, ἄλληκτος, ὀρίνω, ἐρέχθω, and θυμοραϊστής. First, to quote the simile at IX 4–8:

ὡς δ' ἄνεμοι δύο πόντον ὀρίνετον ἰχθυόεντα,
Βορέης καὶ Ζέφυρος, τώ τε Θρήκηθεν ἄητον,
ἐλθόντ', ἐξαπίνης· ἄμυδις δέ τε κῦμα κελαινὸν
κορθύεται, πόλλον δὲ παρὲξ ἅλα φῦκος ἔχευεν·
ὣς ἐδαΐζετο θυμὸς ἐνὶ στήθεσσιν Ἀχαιῶν.

Thus do the two winds Boreas and Zephyr, who blow down from Thrace, stir up the fishy sea, coming suddenly; and a black wave is heaped up in a mass, and seaweed is scattered over the sea far and wide. Even so was the θυμός in the breasts of the Akhaians divided.

The simile spells out the equation, making it possible to appreciate the connection between divine anger and actual stormy weather at XXI 385–388:

---

[5] D. Francis, "Virtue, Folly, and Greek Etymology," *Approaches to Homer*, ed. C. Rubino and C. Shelmerdine, Austin, 1983, 89 ff.
[6] x 1–75.
[7] See Chapter 3, 80. Cf. also Francis.

ἐν δ' ἄλλοισι θεοῖσιν ἔρις πέσε βεβριθυῖα
ἀργαλέη, δίχα δέ σφιν ἐνὶ φρεσὶ θυμὸς ἄητο·
σὺν δ' ἔπεσον μεγάλῳ πατάγῳ, βράχε δ' εὐρεῖα χθών,
ἀμφὶ δὲ σάλπιγξεν μέγας οὐρανός..........

Strife fell among the other gods, extremely harsh, and their θυμός in the φρήν blew asunder. They fell together with a great din, and the wide earth rang, and the great heaven trumpeted round about.

Although the emotional situation in the second passage differs from that in the first, the main point to be made from both is the same: as the winds are roused and blow violently in a storm, so does the θυμός move impetuously within the φρήν/φρένες of the person in conflict.

Passages comparing the winds with θυμός do not occur in large numbers; but there are associations with words having to do with winds and storms which substantiate the evidence in these similes. At the end of Chapter III, it was seen that θυμός dominates the context of motivation, marked particularly by the verbs ὀρίνω, ἀνίημι, ἐποτρύω and ἐπισσεύομαι. These words also occur in the context of weather, a fact which probably accounts for the preference for θυμός over other psychological entities.[8] At XXIII 208–215, Akhilleus prays to Zephyr and Boreas for help in lighting Patroklos' funeral pyre:

"ἀλλ' Ἀχιλεὺς Βορέην ἠδὲ Ζέφυρον κελαδεινὸν
ἐλθεῖν ἀρᾶται, καὶ ὑπίσχεται ἱερὰ καλά,
ὄφρα πυρὴν ὄρσητε καήμεναι, ᾗ ἔνι κεῖται
Πάτροκλ ,ς, τὸν πάντες ἀναστενάχουσιν Ἀχαιοί."
Ἡ μὲν ἄρ' ὣς εἰποῦσ' ἀπεβήσετο, τοὶ δ' ὀρέοντο
ἠχῇ θεσπεσίῃ, νέφεα κλονέοντε πάροιθεν.
αἶψα δὲ πόντον ἵκανον ἀήμεναι, ὦρτο δὲ κῦμα
πνοιῇ ὕπο λιγυρῇ·.....

"But Akhilleus prays that Boreas and blustering Zephyr come, and he promises them fair sacrifices, so that they may rouse the pyre to burn, where Patroklos lies, Patroklos whom all of the Akhaians are mourning." Speaking thus, she went off, and they started up with a great din, driving clouds before them. And they came suddenly to blow upon the sea and raised up a wave with their shrill blast;.....

In the last line, the wave is roused (ὀρίνω) by a blast, or a breath (πνοιή) of the winds which blow (ἄημι) over the πόντος.

At XXI 394–395, boldness is equated with the arousal of the θυμός:

"τίπτ' αὖτ', ὦ κυνάμυια, θεοὺς ἔριδι ξυνελαύνεις
θάρσος ἄητον ἔχουσα, μέγας δέ σε θυμὸς ἀνῆκεν;

"Why again, dog-face, do you drive the gods together in strife, you who have blustering boldness, and (why) has your great θυμός driven you (to it)?

---

[8] See Chapter 3, 81.

Here also a connection is made between strife among the gods and stormy weather. The adjective ἄητος modifying θάρσος is derived from ἄημι, "to blow"; and the verb ἀνίημι is familiar from the context of motivation. Its use in this passage, with the phrase ἄητον θάρσος, suggests a stirring up on the level of cosmic forces.

At ix 136–139, the connection between the human level and the level of cosmic forces is expressed by parallel construction:

ἐν δὲ λιμὴν εὔορμος, ἵν' οὐ χρεὼ πείσματός ἐστιν,
οὔτ' εὐνὰς βαλέειν οὔτε πρυμνήσι' ἀνάψαι,
ἀλλ' ἐπικέλσαντας μεῖναι χρόνον εἰς ὅ κε ναυτέων
θυμὸς ἐποτρύνῃ καὶ ἐπιπνεύσωσιν ἀῆται.

It was a harbor of fair anchorage, where there was no need for stern cables, nor was there need to cast anchor or to tie the prows; we needed only to come into shore and to await the time when the sailor's θυμός would urge and the blasts breathe upon (them).

In other words, the inner motivation is simultaneous with, but not synonymous with, the appropriate weather conditions. Earlier in this chapter, XXI 286 was quoted because the conflict on Olympus is synonymous with conflict on the cosmic level, i.e. a storm. The θυμός blew (ἄητο) asunder within the φρένες, whereas here the blasts (ἀῆται) breathe. The ease with which these words move back and forth between the psychological and the cosmic levels ought also to remind us of V 696–698, where the πνοιή of Boreas revives Sarpedon by breathing upon (ἐπιπνείουσα) him the θυμός which had wafted away (κεκαφηότα).[9] And again I mention xxi 343 (=355), where Penelope puts a μῦθος πεπνυμένος into her θυμός.

At II 292–294, the sea is roused by winds:

καὶ γάρ τίς θ' ἕνα μῆνα μένων ἀπὸ ἧς ἀλόχοιο
ἀσχαλάᾳ σὺν νηὶ πολυζύγῳ, ὅν περ ἄελλαι
χειμέριαι εἰλέωσιν ὀρινομένη τε θάλασσα·

and a man chafes, remaining away from his wife for a month, with the many-benched ship, the man whom winter blasts and the stirred-up sea hold back.

The importance of this passage lies in the fact that the sea is described as stirred up (ὀρινομένη) by blasts (ἄελλαι) by a verb frequently used in the context of motivation with θυμός. Further evidence of this interchangeability lies in XI 296–298, where Hektor falls like a blast of wind into the battle:

αὐτὸς δ' ἐν πρώτοισι μέγα φρονέων ἐβεβήκει
ἐν δ' ἔπεσ' ὑσμίνῃ ὑπεραέϊ ἶσος ἀέλλῃ,
ἥ τε καθαλλομένη ἰοειδέα πόντον ὀρίνει.

---

[9] See Chapter 3, 5. This is to say nothing of the connection made by Nagy of θυμός and its cognates to "the exhaust of sacrificial fire," 1980, 183–184 (#57), substantiated by the fact that the verb καπύειν is used with ψυχή in the context of loss of consciousness/death at XXII 467. Its derivative noun, καπνός is the semantic equivalent of Latin *fumus*, cognate with θυμός.

And he, thinking great thoughts, went into the front lines and fell into the fray like a high-blown blast of wind, which leaping down from above stirs up the blue water.

It should be noted that he is like a blast of wind as he is very active in his φρένες (μέγα φρονέων), and that again it is a blast of wind which stirs up, in this case the πόντος.[10]

In several passages, the verb ὀρίνω occurs only on the cosmic level. For instance, at XXI 311–315, the river Xanthos appeals to the Simoeis to help him defeat Akhilleus:

ἀλλ' ἐπάμυνε τάχιστα, καὶ ἐμπίπληθι ῥέεθρα
ὕδατος ἐκ πηγέων, πάντας δ' ὀρόθυνον ἐναύλους,
ἵστη δὲ μέγα κῦμα, πολὺν δ' ὀρυμαγδὸν ὄρινε
φιτρῶν καὶ λαῶν, ἵνα παύσομεν ἄγριον ἄνδρα,
ὃς δὴ νῦν κρατέει, μέμονεν δ' ὅ γε ἶσα θεοῖσι.

But ward him off quickly, and fill your streams with water from the springs, and set in motion all your torrents, and raise up a big wave, and stir up a great din of timbers and rocks, so that we may stop the wild man, who now prevails, and rages like the gods.

Here the forces of nature are needed to withstand the might of a man who rages like the gods (cosmic forces). At II 142–146, θυμός is compared to a storm wind when aroused:

ὣς φάτο, τοῖσι δὲ θυμὸν ἐνὶ στήθεσσιν ὄρινε
πᾶσι μετὰ πληθύν, ὅσοι οὐ βουλῆς ἐπάκουσαν·
κινήθη δ' ἀγορὴ φὴ κύματα μακρὰ θαλάσσης,
πόντου Ἰκαρίοιο, τὰ μέν τ' Εὖρός τε Νότος τε
ὤρορ' ἐπαΐξας πατρὸς Διὸς ἐκ νεφελάων.

Thus he spoke, and the θυμός in the breasts of all the men throughout the gathering was roused up, as many as who did not heed the plan. And the assembly was moved like great waves on the sea, the Icarian Sea, waves which the East and South Winds raise, having struck down from the clouds of Father Zeus.

Two more short passages demonstrate the interchangeability of vocabulary between the two levels. At viii 178, there is an expression of inner motivation:

ὤρινάς μοι θυμὸν ἐνὶ στήθεσσιν φίλοισιν

You have roused up the θυμός in my breast . . . . .

and at vii 273, the same verb is used of a storm at sea:

ὤρινεν δὲ θάλασσαν ἀθέσφατον, ...

. . . . . he (Poseidon) stirred up an unspeakable sea . . . . .

---

[10] See other passages quoted in Chapter 3, 80.

The use of the adjective ἄλληκτος illustrates the same point. It is used rarely with θυμός and also with a wind. An example of the former occurs at IX 636–638:

> .... σοὶ δ' ἄλληκτόν τε κακόν τε
> θυμὸν ἐνὶ στήθεσσι θεοὶ θέσαν εἵνεκα κούρης οἴης: ....[11]

The gods put an unceasing and evil θυμός in your breast on account of one girl ...

Then at xii 325, the same adjective is used to describe the South Wind:

> μῆνα δὲ πάντ' ἄλληκτος ἄη Νότος, ...

The South Wind blew unceasing for the whole month, ...

There are a number of other passages in the Homeric poems which illustrate the same point,[12] and it is apparent from the similes as well as from the coincidence in vocabulary that θυμός, though treated as a psychological entity, was seen to behave like a wind but on the human level. Significantly, it is Akhilleus' θυμός which blows ceaselessly in one particular direction, for he himself has close associations with the wind, as can be seen from XXII 208–215 where he summons the winds to light Patroklos' pyre. And as Nagy points out in *The Best of the Achaeans*,[13] Akhilleus as Ποντάρχης presided over a cult on the Hellespont.

Next the word θύω should be considered in both contexts. It is not used with θυμός itself but does occur in passages describing the inner state of an individual, usually without the inclusion of a psychological entity; and it also occurs in descriptions of the elements. At I 342–344, Akhilleus describes Agamemnon's witlessness thus:

> ".......... ἦ γὰρ ὅ γ' ὀλοιῇσι φρεσὶ θύει,
> οὐδέ τι οἶδε νοῆσαι ἅμα πρόσσω καὶ ὀπίσσω,
> ὅππως οἱ παρὰ νηυσὶ σόοι μαχέοιντο Ἀχαιοί."

> .... indeed he rages within his deadly φρένες, nor did he know how to look ahead and back at the same time, how the Akhaians might fight safely beside the ships.

This passage makes a perfect case for Plato's etymology, particularly because the activity θύω is located φρεσί. This is the only example where the

---

[11] Note that κακός is used of unfavorable winds, e.g. at VI 346.
[12] III 395, IV 208, V 29, XI 804, XIII 468, XIV 459, 487, XV 403, XVI 280, XVII 123, XVIII 223, XXIV 467, 568; iv 366, xiv 361, xv 486, xvii 150, xviii 75, xx 9, xxi 87, xxiv 318.
[13] Nagy 1979, 340 ff. Also, see Nagy, *Arethusa* 16.1–2 (1983), 50 on the connection of σῆμα το νόησις· "Or again, there is the σῆμα of Achilles and Patroklos at the Hellespont, which is τηλεφανής 'shining from afar' as a beacon of salvation for sailors at sea (xxiv 80–84, in conjunction with XIX 374–380)."

location is specified, but there are three other passages in the *Iliad* where it describes an intense inner state,[14] the first at XXI 234-236:

> .... ὁ δ' ἐπέσσυτο οἴδματι θύων,
> πάντα δ' ὄρινε ῥέεθρα κυκώμενος, ὦσε δὲ νεκροὺς
> πολλούς, οἵ ῥα κατ' αὐτὸν ἅλις ἔσαν, οὓς κτάν' Ἀχιλλεύς·

But he (Xanthos) rushed upon him, raging with his swell, and heaping up all his streams, he rose up, and he pushed many dead men, who were too many for him, the men whom Akhilles had slain.

A little further on, at XXI 324-325, the same picture is presented again:

> Ἦ, καὶ ἐπῶρτ' Ἀχιλῆϊ κυκώμενος, ὑψόσε θύων,
> μορμύρων ἀφρῷ τε καὶ αἵματι νεκύεσσι.

He spoke, and stirring up rose against Akhilleus, raging from above, roaring with foam and blood and dead bodies.

In both the above passages, it is the water which rages; and in the description of Patroklos' pyre being lit by the winds, the sea rages — but under the blasts of the wind, as at XXIII 229-230:

> οἱ δ' ἄνεμοι πάλιν αὖτις ἔβαν οἰκόνδε νέεσθαι
> Θρηΐκιον κατὰ πόντον· ὁ δ' ἔστενεν οἴδματι θύων.

The winds again went back home over the Thracian sea; and it groaned, raging with its swell.[15]

In the *Odyssey*, θύω is used consistently to describe the effect of the winds upon water, as in the *Iliad*, or of wind itself, as at xiii 84-85:

> ὣς ἄρα τῆς πρύμνη μὲν ἀείρετο, κῦμα δ' ὄπισθε
> πορφύρεον μέγα θῦε πολυφλοίσβοιο θαλάσσης.

thus indeed her (the ship's) stern was raised, and the great purple wave of the loud-roaring sea boiled up behind.

At xii 400:

> καὶ τότ' ἔπειτ' ἄνεμος μὲν ἐπαύσατο λαίλαπι θύων,

..... and then when the wind ceased raging with the storm .....

At xii 407-410, the storm resumes:

> .... αἶψα γὰρ ἦλθε
> κεκληγὼς Ζέφυρος, μεγάλῃ σὺν λαίλαπι θύων,
> ἱστοῦ δὲ προτόνους ἔρρηξ' ἀνέμοιο θύελλα
> ἀμφοτέρους ....

---

[14] XI 180, XVI 699, XXII 272.
[15] See Chapter 3, 33; also IX 549-550.

> Zephyr returned roaring, raging with a great storm, and the blast of wind broke the mast stays, both of them, ...

It is clear then that θύω is related semantically to θυμός and that it strengthens the case for synonymity between the level of the individual and the cosmic level of the elements.

The verb ἐρέχθω is used only three times in Homeric diction; and significantly, the passages fit exactly into the two contexts discussed above. At XXIII 316–317, it is used to describe a storm-battered ship:

> μήτι δ' αὖτε κυβερνήτης ἐνὶ οἴνοπι πόντῳ
> νῆα θοὴν ἰθύνει ἐρεχθομένην ἀνέμοισι·
>
> It is with skill that the pilot guides his wind-battered ship on the wine-dark sea;
> . . . . .

This little aphorism occurs in the midst of a speech of advice given by Nestor to his son Antilokhos on how to win the chariot race. At v 82–84,[16] Odysseus weeps over his difficulties:

> ἀλλ' ὅ γ' ἐπ' ἀκτῆς κλαῖε καθήμενος, ἔνθα πάρος περ,
> δάκρυσι καὶ στοναχῇσι καὶ ἄλγεσι θυμὸν ἐρέχθων.
> πόντον ἐπ' ἀτρύγετον δερκέσκετο δάκρυα λείβων.
>
> but he sat weeping upon a promontory, there where he had sat before, lacerating his θυμός with tears and groans and griefs. He was gazing down upon the barren sea pouring down tears.

The disparity between the two comparisons exists in the fact that the wind batters in the first passage, and in the second the θυμός is battered. However, it must be significant that in the second, or metaphorical, passage epic diction has maintained a connection with the concrete meaning of ἐρέχθω by placing Odysseus on a promontory overlooking the sea.

The adjective θυμοραϊστής must be mentioned not only because of its significance in relation to θυμός but because of its connection with the compound verb διαρραίω.[17] The adjective occurs five times in the *Iliad*, three times to describe death[18] and twice to describe enemies.[19] The compound verb is used a number of times in the *Iliad* to describe complete destruction.[20] Death tears apart and scatters the θυμός in the same way that winds destroy a ship at sea. As with ἐρέχθω, the comparison is not entirely balanced: although θυμός is visualized as behaving like a wind, it is also visualized as being scattered as though by winds. This irrevocable scattering

---

[16] v 83–84 =157–158.
[17] Chantraine, 965, "briser, écraser, dit notamment pour un naufrage."
[18] XIII 544, XVI 414, 580.
[19] XVI 591, XVIII 220.
[20] II 473, IX 78, XI 713, XVII 727, XXIV 355.

or separation which takes place at death is directly opposed to its regathering into the φρήν/φρένες of the person who has regained consciousness.[21]

The verb ἐπισσεύομαι, finally, also occurs on both the individual and the cosmic levels. It is used four times in the *Iliad* to describe the movement of θυμός but occurs even more frequently in descriptions of the swift movement of warriors in battle.[22] The passage at XXI 234 has already been quoted above in connection with θύω. At XVII 736–739, the onslaught of fire is compared to the rush of battle:

> ....ἐπὶ δὲ πτόλεμος τέτατό σφιν
> ἄγριος ἠΰτε πῦρ, τό τ' ἐπεσσύμενον πόλιν ἀνδρῶν
> ὄρμενον ἐξαίφνης φλέγεθει, μινύθουσι δὲ οἶκοι
> ἐν σέλαϊ μεγάλῳ· τὸ δ' ἐπιβρέμει ἲς ἀνέμοιο.

and the fierce battle reached toward them like a fire, which, rushing on, suddenly rising sets a town of men ablaze, and the houses are consumed in the great conflagration; and the might of the winds fans it to a great roar.

The movement is swift and irresistible. Something of this force is present also in passages where ἐπισσεύομαι is used with θυμός. At I 173, the connotations of the verb make Agamemnon's remark to Akhilleus thoroughly insulting:

> "φεῦγε μάλ', εἴ τοι θυμὸς ἐπέσσυται, ..."
>
> "Flee, then, if your θυμός drives you to it ....."

And as Hektor takes leave of Helen at VI 361–362, he excuses his haste thus:

> ἤδη γάρ μοι θυμὸς ἐπέσσυται ὄφρ' ἐπαμύνω
> Τρώεσσ', ...
>
> for already my θυμός has driven me to defend the Trojans, ...

At IX 42–43, Diomedes encourages Agamemnon to return home:

> εἰ δέ τοι αὐτῷ θυμὸς ἐπέσσυται ὥς τε νέεσθαι,
>
> but if your θυμός has driven you to return, come: .....

And at IX 398–400, Akhilleus speaks of his longing to lead a different life:

> ἔνθα δέ μοι μάλα πολλὸν ἐπέσσυτο θυμὸς ἀγήνωρ
> γήμαντι μνηστὴν ἄλοχον, εἰκυῖαν ἄκοιτιν
> κτήμασι τέρπεσθαι τὰ γέρων ἐκτήσατο Πηλεύς·
>
> My manly θυμός has been driving me there, having wed a lawful wife, a bride to my liking, to enjoy the property which the aged Peleus has amassed.

The bridge between the two levels can be seen in XXI 227:[23]

---

[21] Cf. XXII 475.
[22] II 86, 208, XIII 757, XV 593, XVIII 575.
[23] See also V 438, 459, 884, XVI 705, XX 447, XXI 227.

60 ΘΥΜΟΣ EXAMINED FURTHER: CONNECTIONS WITH THE WINDS

ὣς εἰπὼν Τρώεσσιν ἐπέσσυτο δαίμονι ἶσος:

Speaking thus, he rushed upon the Trojans like a δαίμων.

In battle men move like higher powers, swiftly, forcefully, irresistibly; and behind this movement is the force of the θυμός which is a piece as it were of the elements on loan to the individual.

Many passages have been cited for the purpose of demonstrating the connection of θυμός with the winds, a connection which is characteristic for it alone of the psychological entities in epic diction. The occurrence of θυμός alone out of the varied psychological vocabulary can be explained in certain connections by this association with the wind, as for example with the words ἄημι, ὀρίνω, ἐπισσεύομαι, and ἐρέχθω. The adjectives ἄλληκτος and θυμοραϊστής, though infrequent, also belong in this group. Equally significant is the relationship of θυμός to φρήν/φρένες on the level of the individual, for it has its cosmic counterpart in the story of Odysseus' struggle with the winds given to him in bags by Aiolos: θυμός, like the winds, become destructive and uncontrollable when not properly contained, blowing the individual figuratively or the ship literally off course.

The validity of this last connection has been recently confirmed by E. D. Francis in an article dealing with the problem of the etymology of ἄτη.[24] By reconstructing a formal connection between the verbs ἀάζω and ἄημι, he is able to connect the noun ἄτη not only with the former verb but with the latter. The crucial passage, XXI 385–386, substantiates the semantic connection, as we have already seen. And at xxi 301–302, three derivatives of ἄημι occur in a psychological context:

.... ὁ δὲ φρεσὶν ᾗσιν ἀασθεὶς
ἤϊεν ἣν ἄτην ὀχέων ἀεσίφρονι θυμῷ.

.... but he, having gone astray in his φρένες, went off holding this error in his blasted θυμός.

It is close to impossible to translate the passage in a way that gives the true sense of the epic diction, in large part because the idea of being blown off course is repeated three times in relation to the φρένες and the θυμός, by the verb ἀάζω, the noun ἄτη and the adjective ἀεσίφρων, which is derived from the verb ἄημι. It is particularly ironic that the suitors threaten the disguised Odysseus with this description of the fate of the Centaur Eurytion; Odysseus is so well disguised, apparently, that not a shred of his legendary νόος is in evidence, and it is the suitors who in fact are being blown off course.

Furthermore, the cosmic-psychological connection already exists in the

---

[24] E. D. Francis, 1983, 89–103.

Latin cognates of Greek ἄνεμος, "wind", in *animus* "soul" and *anima* "breeze". It is not surprising, therefore, that Latin *fumus* should mean "smoke" or "that which is blown on a breeze" and Greek θυμός "soul", "life-soul", or "that which animates and endows the human being with consciousness, air blown into the lungs by the winds".[25] And it should no longer require a leap of faith to accept the use of the adjective πεπνυμένος in descriptions of acts or words performed with the benefit of breathing consciousness, hence intelligence. This synonymity between the winds and θυμός was buried gradually by the tendency of the language to specialize and draw distinctions between the cosmic and the individual levels. But because epic diction is conservative, it is still possible to discover the remnants of this relationship.

CONCLUSION

At the end of Chapter III, it had become apparent that θυμός, although frequently a functional synonym for other psychological terms, is given specific characteristics by epic diction which it does not share with those terms. To summarize briefly the findings on the usage of these words: in the context of loss of consciousness/death, only θυμός returns to the person who is revived. And only the ψυχή arrives at Hades after death, at which point θυμός is dissipated. During consciousness, θυμός normally resides in the φρήν/φρένες. Its strength is in part connected to the physical condition and circumstances of the body, thus making the emotional state of the individual somewhat dependent on his physical condition. In its proper state, θυμός is described as *not* rigid but flexible, since it blows (ἄημι) inwardly.

In the context of the intellect, it is used much less often than other terms, such as φρήν/φρένες and νόος, and may be included to indicate an admixture of emotion seen as being present in a situation which is also cognitive. Here in occasional passages, it is implicit in the language of the poems that for the intellect to function properly, θυμός needs to be contained by the φρήν/φρένες. In a number of passages examined, the failure of the intellect to function properly is a result of the θυμός passing outside the limit of the φρένες and thus figuratively blowing the individual off course. And as breathing brings consciousness, during which state the θυμός is in the φρήν/φρένες, it is also seen to produce an intelligent (πεπνυμένος) speech or thought. Onians' conclusion that φρήν/φρένες can be equated with the lungs and diaphragm fits in well with the evidence produced here. It is also significant in this context that the φρήν/φρένες and θυμός be of the appropriate respective consistencies, i.e. close-knit and thus containing and

---

[25] Cf. xxi 302.

flexible and thus capable of fitting into a container. Understandably the state of the container is crucial in this context, partially explaining why the φρήν/ φρένες plays a dominant role.

In the context of the emotions, θυμός dominates its functional synonyms, outnumbering φρήν/φρένες, the next most frequently-used term, which, however, occurs often as the location rather than the entity acting or acted upon directly. Θυμός is used with such a wide range of verbs and nouns denoting different emotions that it itself clearly has to be considered as without affiliations to any specific emotions. Again in this context, the containment of θυμός indicates controlled emotion, whereas uncontained θυμός results in extreme behavior.

In the context of inner debate, the fact that θυμός and φρήν/φρένες are used frequently together suggests that this state is considered both emotional and intellectual from the point of view of epic diction. And in the context of motivation, θυμός has varied and numerous associations with the language of winds and storms. The convergence of vocabulary with that of winds and storms helps explain the concept of containment of the θυμός within the φρήν/φρένες. Odysseus' struggle with the winds of Aiolos, where lack of containment leads to disaster, is taken as the parallel on the cosmic level.

The findings of Chapters III and IV thus offer a very clear if untranslatable idea of the nature of θυμός. What, then, is it? The word "soul" is of course completely inappropriate because of its eschatological associations; and even the term "life-soul" does not adequately express its characteristics. Modern English can supply no better than a crude approximation, either linguistically or conceptually. In the diction of early Greek epic, θυμός forms the basis of consciousness and thus of all internal experiences and also possesses certain definite characteristics which are allied very closely to the nature of the winds. Its strength is closely connected with the physical condition of the body and also helps determine how the individual functions intellectually and emotionally. This partaking of the physical and the psychical defies description but is also totally in keeping with the other glimpses given us of early Greek psychology by the Homeric poems. I submit that θυμός is in fact the human counterpart of the winds, brought to animate the body by the winds as we see in the revival of Sarpedon, and carried away on the winds from the body once it has ceased to be able, for whatever reason, physically to continue breathing and to contain the θυμός within the φρήν/φρένες.

On the basis of this definition, it seems clear that θυμός can be derived not only formally but semantically from θύω. On the cosmic level, its counterpart is θύελλα, just as Latin has its *animus/anima*, cognates of Greek ἄνεμος. In a development parallel with that of ψυχή "soul" from ψύχω "to blow, breathe," θυμός "inner wind, bearer of consciousness, energy, and experience" arose from θύω, "to rush, run, flow." It can be supposed that in the process of semantic specialization, despite the fact that their origins are so similar, θυμός came to refer only to the inner functions of the living person, whereas ψυχή came to refer to the entity which survives death. And as is known from the literature of classical times, the meaning of θυμός continued to change, ceasing to be connected with *all* inner experiences of whatever nature, but coming to signify in particular violent emotion. It is easy to see how this change came about, since the containment of θυμός, often an implied condition to normal functioning, necessarily has its more violent and perhaps more interesting counterpart. The force inherent in the basic concept is given to us not only in the parable of Odysseus and the winds, but in the literally stormy contexts where θύω and θύελλα are generally found. As so often in epic diction, the manifestations and experiences of the individual are pieces of a greater whole, significant in the world of men but also indissolubly connected with the cosmos. It is for this relatedness to the all, this freshness and vitality, that the thought of the early Greeks, and the Homeric poems as examples of that thought, should be considered primitive in the best sense of the word.

APPENDIX

I. Passages Containing Verbs, Nouns and Adjectives of Emotion, Chapter 3, Sections 38–66

ἀνδάνω

I	24	ἀλλ' οὐκ 'Ατρεΐδῃ 'Αγαμέμνονι <u>ἥνδανε θυμῷ</u>,
	378	
XV	674	Οὐδ' ἄρ' ἔτ' Αἴαντι μεγαλήτορι <u>ἥνδανε θυμῷ</u>
xiv	337	........τοῖσιν δὲ κακὴ <u>φρεσὶν ἥνδανε</u> βουλὴ

γήθω

I	255	ἦ κεν <u>γηθήσαι</u> Πρίαμος Πριάμοιό τε παῖδες
	256	ἄλλοι τε Τρῶες μέγα κεν κεχαροίατο <u>θυμῷ</u>,
VII	189	γνῶ δὲ κλήρου σῆμα ἰδών, <u>γήθησε δὲ θυμῷ</u>.
VIII	376	........................ὄφρα ἴδωμαι
	377	ἣ νῶϊ Πριάμοιο πάϊς κορυθαίολος Ἕκτωρ
	378	<u>γηθήσει</u> προφανέντε ἀνὰ πτολέμοιο γεφύρας,
	559	πάντα δὲ εἴδεται ἄστρα, <u>γέγηθε δέ τε φρένα</u> ποιμήν·
IX	77	....................τίς ἂν τάδε <u>γηθήσειε</u>;
XI	683	................<u>γεγήθει δὲ φρένα</u> Νηλεύς,
XIII	343	.... μάλα κεν θρασυκάρδιος εἴη
	344	ὅς τότε <u>γηθήσειεν</u> ἰδὼν πόνον οὐδ' ἀκάχοιτο
	414	.... ἀλλά ἕ φημι
	415	εἰς Ἀϊδός περ ἰόντα πυλάρταο κρατεροῖο
	416	<u>γηθήσειν κατὰ θυμόν</u>, ἐπεὶ ῥά οἱ ὤπασα πομπόν.
	494	ὣς Αἰνείᾳ <u>θυμὸς ἐνὶ στήθεσσι γεγήθει</u>,
XIV	139	'Ατρεΐδη, νῦν δή που 'Αχιλλῆος ὀλοὸν <u>κῆρ</u>
	140	<u>γηθεῖ ἐνὶ στήθεσσι</u>,..................
XVI	530	Γλαῦκος δῷ ἔγνω <u>ᾗσιν ἐνὶ φρεσὶ γήθησέν τε</u>,
XVII	567	Ὣς φάτο, <u>γήθησεν</u> δὲ θεὰ γλαυκῶπις Ἀθήνη,
XXIV	320	.... οἱ δὲ ἰδόντες
	321	<u>γήθησαν, καὶ πᾶσιν ἐνὶ φρεσὶ θυμὸς</u> ἰάνθη.
	424	Ὣς φάτο, <u>γήθησεν</u> δ ὁ γέρων, καὶ ἀμείβετο μύθῳ·
vi	106	................<u>γέγηθε</u> δέ τε <u>φρένα</u> Λητώ
vii	269	............<u>γήθησε</u> δέ μοι φίλον <u>ἦτορ</u>
viii	385	Ὣς φάτο· <u>γήθησεν</u> δ' ἱερὸν <u>μένος</u> 'Αλκινόοιο.
Theog	173	.........<u>γήθησεν</u> δὲ μέγα <u>φρεσὶ</u> Γαῖα πελώρη·
Sc.H.	115	.... μείδησεν δὲ βίη Ἡρακληείη
	116	<u>θυμῷ γηθήσας</u>.....................
H. Dem.	232	.................<u>γεγήθει δὲ φρένα</u> μήτηρ.
H.Aphr.	216	.... <u>γεγήθει δὲ φρένας</u> ἔνδον,
	217	<u>γηθόσυνος</u> δ' ἵπποισιν ἀελλοπόδεσσιν ὀχεῖτο.

γηθοσύνη

XIII	29	<u>γηθοσύνῃ</u> δὲ θάλασσα διίστατο............
XXI	389	................ἐγέλασσε δέ οἱ φίλον <u>ἦτορ</u>
	390	<u>γηθοσύνῃ</u>,................................

γηθόσυνος

IV	272	Ὣς ἔφατ', 'Ατρεΐδης δὲ παρῴχετο <u>γηθόσυνος κῆρ</u>·
	326	
XVIII	556	...................βασιλεὺς δ' ἐν τοῖσι σιωπῇ
	557	σκῆπτρον ἔχων ἑστήκει ἐπ' ὄγμου <u>γηθόσυνος κῆρ</u>.

βούλομαι

XII	174	Ἕκτορι γάρ οἱ <u>θυμὸς ἐβούλετο</u> κῦδος ὀρέξαι.
XV	596	

H.Apol.	532	.... οἳ μελεδῶνας
	533	βούλεσθ' ἀργαλέους τε πόνους καὶ στείνεα θυμῷ·

μενοινάω

XIV	221	.... ὅ τι φρεσὶ σῇσι μενοινᾷς.
	264	Ὕπνε, τίη δὲ σὺ ταῦτα μετὰ φρεσὶ σῇσι μενοινᾷς;
XIX	164	εἴ περ γὰρ θυμῷ γε μενοινάᾳ πολεμίζειν,
ii	33	.... εἴθε οἱ αὐτῷ
	34	Ζεὺς ἀγαθὸν τελέσειεν, ὅ τι φρεσὶν ᾗσι μενοινᾷ.
	248	ἐξελάσαι μεγάροιο μενοινήσει' ἐνὶ θυμῷ,
vi	180	σοὶ δὲ θεοὶ τόσα δοῖεν ὅσα φρεσὶ σῇσι μενοινᾷς,
xv	111	Τηλέμαχ', ἦ τοι νόστον, ὅπως φρεσὶ σῇσι μενοινᾷς,

τιτύσκομαι

XIII	558	.... τιτύσκετο δὲ φρεσὶν ᾗσιν
	559	ἤ τευ ἀκοντίσσαι, ἠὲ σχεδὸν ὁρμηθῆναι.
viii	556	ὄφρα σε τῇ πέμπωσι τιτυσκόμεναι φρεσὶ νῆες.

ἵεμαι

II	589	.... μάλιστα δὲ ἵετο θυμῷ
	590	τείσασθαι Ἑλένης ὁρμήματά τε στοναχάς τε.
VIII	301	.... βαλέειν δέ ἑ ἵετο θυμός·
	310	
XIII	386	....................ὁ δὲ ἵετο θυμῷ
	387	Ἰδομενῆα βαλεῖν·....................

χαίρω

I	256	ἄλλοι τε Τρῶες μέγα κεν κεχαροίατο θυμῷ,
V	243	Τυδεΐδη Διόμηδες, ἐμῷ κεχαρισμένε θυμῷ,
	826	
X	234	
VI	480	................φέροι δ' ἔναρα βροτόεντα
	481	κτείνας δήϊον ἄνδρα, χαρείη δὲ φρένα μήτηρ.
VII	191	ᾧ φίλοι, ἤτοι κλῆρος ἐμός, χαίρω δὲ καὶ αὐτὸς
	192	θυμῷ, ἐπεὶ δοκέω νικησέμεν Ἕκτορα δῖον.
XI	608	δῖε Μενοιτιάδη, τῷ ἐμῷ κεχαρισμένε θυμῷ,
XIII	609	.....ὁ δὲ φρεσὶν ᾗσι χάρη καὶ ἐέλπετο νίκην.
XIV	156	.... χαῖρε δὲ θυμῷ·
XV	97	....................οὐδέ τί φημι
	98	πᾶσιν ὁμῶς θυμὸν κεχαρησέμεν,...........
XIX	287	Πάτροκλέ μοι δειλῇ πλεῖστον κεχαρισμένε θυμῷ,
XXI	423	Ὣς φάτ', Ἀθηναίη δὲ μετέσσυτο, χαῖρε δὲ θυμῷ,
XXII	224	Ὣς φάτ' Ἀθηναίη, ὁ δ' ἐπείθετο, χαῖρε δὲ θυμῷ,
xxiv	545	
XXIV	490	ἀλλ' ἤτοι κεῖνός γε σέθεν ζώοντος ἀκούων
	491	χαίρει τῷ ἐν θυμῷ,.....................
i	311	δῶρον ἔχων ἐπὶ νῆα κίῃς, χαίρων ἐνὶ θυμῷ,
iv	71	Φράζεο, Νεστορίδη, τῷ ἐμῷ κεχαρισμένε θυμῷ,
	259	.........................αὐτὰρ ἐμὸν κῆρ
	260	χαῖρ', ἐπεὶ ἤδη μοι κραδίη τέτραπτο νέεσθαι
vi	23	ἥ οἱ ὁμηλικίη μὲν ἔην, κεχάριστο δὲ θυμῷ.
viii	78	.... ἄναξ δῷ ἀνδρῶν Ἀγαμέμνων
	79	χαῖρε νόῳ, ὅ τ' ἄριστοι Ἀχαιῶν δηριόωντο.
	394	.....................ὄφρ' ἐνὶ χερσὶ
	395	ξεῖνος ἔχων ἐπὶ δόρπον ἵῃ χαίρων ἐνὶ θυμῷ.
	483	.... ὁ δ' ἐδέξατο, χαῖρε δὲ θυμῷ.
xiv	113	.... ὁ δ' ἐδέξατο, χαῖρε δὲ θυμῷ
xxii	411	ἐν θυμῷ, γρηῦ, χαῖρε καὶ ἴσχεο μηδ' ὀλόλυζε·
xxiii	266	οὔ μέν τοι θυμὸς κεχαρήσεται.............
Erga	683	..... οὐ γὰρ ἐμῷ θυμῷ κεχαρισμένος ἐστίν·

APPENDIX

H.Dem.	458	ἀσπασίως δ' ἴδον ἀλλήλας, <u>κεχάρηντο</u> δὲ <u>θυμῷ</u>.
H.Herm.	520	πάντ' ἂν ἐμῷ <u>θυμῷ</u> <u>κεχαρισμένα</u> καὶ φίλα ἔρδοις.
H.Dion.	55	θάρσει, †δῖε κάτωρ† τῷ ἐμῷ <u>κεχαρισμένε</u> <u>θυμῷ</u>·

τέρπω/τέρπομαι

XIX	19	αὐτὰρ ἐπεὶ <u>φρεσὶν</u> ᾖσι <u>τετάρπετο</u> δαίδαλα λεύσσων,
	312	...........................οὐδέ τι <u>θυμῷ</u>
	313	<u>τέρπετο</u>,................................
XX	23	ἥμενος, ἔνθ' ὁρόων φρένα <u>τέρψομαι</u>·..........
XXI	45	ἕνδεκα δ' ἤματα <u>θυμὸν</u> <u>ἐτέρπετο</u> οἷσι φίλοισιν
	46	ἐλθὼν ἐκ Λήμνοιο·......................
i	106	..........................οἱ μὲν ἔπειτα
	107	πεσσοῖσι προπάροιθε θυράων <u>θυμὸν</u> <u>ἔτερπον</u>,
iv	102	ἄλλοτε μέν τε γόῳ <u>φρένα</u> <u>τέρπομαι</u>,..........
viii	367	......................αὐτὰρ Ὀδυσσεὺς
	368	<u>τέρπετ'</u> ἐνὶ <u>φρεσὶν</u> ᾗσιν ἀκούων ἠδὲ καὶ ἄλλοι
xxi	105	αὐτὰρ ἐγὼ γελόω καὶ <u>τέρπομαι</u> ἄφρονι <u>θυμῷ</u>.
Erga	57	........................ᾧ κεν ἅπαντες
	58	<u>τέρπωνται</u> κατὰ <u>θυμόν</u>, ἑὸν κακὸν ἀμφαγαπῶντες.
	357	ὃς μὲν γάρ κεν ἀνὴρ ἐθέλων ὅ γε καὶ μέγα δώῃ,
	358	<u>χαίρει</u> τῷ δώρῳ καὶ <u>τέρπεται</u> ὃν κατὰ <u>θυμόν</u>·
Theog.	36	τύνη, Μουσάων ἀρχώμεθα, ταὶ Διὶ πατρὶ
	37	ὑμνεῦσαι <u>τέρπουσι</u> μέγα <u>νόον</u> ἐντὸς Ὀλύμπου,
	51	
H.Apol.	341	....................ἣ δὲ ἰδοῦσα
	342	<u>τέρπετο</u> ὃν κατὰ <u>θυμόν</u>, ὀίετο γὰρ τελέεσθαι.
H.Herm.	564	.... σὺ δ' ἀτρεκέως ἐρεείνων
	565	σὴν αὐτοῦ <u>φρένα</u> <u>τέρπε</u>,.................
H. Aphr.	72	.....ἣ δ' ὁρόωσα μετὰ <u>φρεσὶ</u> <u>τέρπετο</u> θυμὸν
	73	καὶ τοῖς ἐν στήθεσσι βάλ' ἵμερον,..........
H.Pan.	45	.........πάντες δ' ἄρα <u>θυμὸν</u> <u>ἔτερφθεν</u>
	46	ἀθάνατοι, περίαλλα δ' ὁ Βάκχειος Διόνυσος·
	47	Πᾶνα δέ μιν καλέεσκον, ὅτι <u>φρένα</u> πᾶσιν <u>ἔτερψε</u>.

ἔλπομαι

X	355	<u>ἔλπετο</u> γὰρ κατὰ <u>θυμὸν</u> ἀποστρέψοντας ἑταίρους
	356	ἐκ Τρώων ἰέναι,....................
XII	407	ἐπεὶ οἱ <u>θυμὸς</u> <u>ἐέλπετο</u> κῦδος ἀρέσθαι.
XIII	8	οὐ γὰρ ὅ γ' ἀθανάτων τινα <u>ἔλπετο</u> ὃν κατὰ <u>θυμὸν</u>
	9	ἐλθόντ' ἢ Τρώεσσιν ἀρηξέμεν ἢ Δαναοῖσιν.
	813	ἦ θήν πού τοι <u>θυμὸς</u> <u>ἐέλπεται</u> ἐξαλαπάζειν
	814	νῆας·..............................
XIV	67	................<u>ἔλποντο</u> δὲ <u>θυμῷ</u>
	68	ἄρρηκτον νηῶν τε καὶ αὐτῶν εἶλαρ ἔσεσθαι·
XV	288	ἦ θήν μιν μάλα <u>ἔλπετο</u> <u>θυμὸς</u> ἑκάστου
	289	χερσὶν ὑπ' Αἴαντος θανέειν Τελαμωνιάδαο.
	701	Τρωσὶν δ' <u>ἔλπετο</u> <u>θυμὸς</u> ἐνὶ στήθεσσιν ἑκάστου
	702	νῆας ἐνιπρήσειν κτενέειν θ' ἥρωας Ἀχαιούς.
XVII	395	......μάλα δέ σφισιν <u>ἔλπετο</u> θυμός,
	404	................τό μιν οὔ ποτε <u>ἔλπετο</u> <u>θυμῷ</u>
	405	τεθνάμεν,...........................
	495	................μάλα δέ σφισιν <u>ἔλπετο</u> <u>θυμὸς</u>
	496	αὐτῷ τε κτενέειν ἐλάαν τῷ ἐριαύχενας ἵππους·
	603	..................ἐπεὶ οὐκέτι <u>ἔλπετο</u> <u>θυμῷ</u>
	604	ἔγχος ἔχων ἐν χειρὶ μαχήσεσθαι Τρώεσσιν.
XIX	328	πρὶν μέν γάρ μοι <u>θυμὸς</u> ἐνὶ στήθεσσιν <u>ἐώλπει</u>
XXI	583	ἦ δή που μάλ' <u>ἔολπας</u> ἐνὶ <u>φρεσί</u>, φαίδιμ' Ἀχιλλεῦ,
iii	275	..................ὃ οὔ ποτε <u>ἔλπετο</u> <u>θυμῷ</u>
ix	419	οὕτω γάρ πού μ' <u>ἤλπετ'</u> ἐνὶ <u>φρεσὶ</u> νήπιον εἶναι.
xx	328	ὄφρα μὲν ὑμῖν <u>θυμὸς</u> ἐνὶ στήθεσσιν <u>ἐώλπει</u>

xxi	329	νοστήσειν Ὀδυσῆα πολύφρονα ὅνδε δόμονδε,
	96	τῷ δ' ἄρα θυμὸς ἐνὶ στήθεσσιν ἐώλπει
	97	.... νευρὴν ἐντανύειν διοϊστεύσειν τε σιδήρου.
	157	νῦν μέν τις καὶ ἔλπετ' ἐνὶ φρεσὶν ἠδὲ μενοινᾷ
	158	γῆμαι Πηνελόπειαν,......................
xxiii	345	ὁππότε δή ῥ' Ὀδυσῆα ἐέλπετο ὃν κατὰ θυμὸν
	346	εὐνῆς ἧς ἀλόχου ταρπήμεναι ἠδὲ καὶ ὕπνου,
xxiv	313	.... θυμὸς δ' ἔτι νῶϊν ἐώλπει
	314	μίξεσθαι ξενίῃ ἠδ' ἀγλαὰ δῶρα διδώσειν.

ἐθέλω

IX	177	
iii	342	
	395	
vii	184	αὐτὰρ ἐπεὶ σπεῖσάν τ' ἔπιόν θ' ὅσον ἤθελε θυμός,
	228	
xviii	427	
XVI	255	........................ἔτι δ' ἤθελε θυμῷ
	256	εἰσιδέειν Τρώων καὶ Ἀχαιῶν φύλοπιν αἰνήν.
XVII	488	.... εἰ σύ γε θυμῷ
	489	σῷ ἐθέλεις,........................
	702	........................ἤθελε θυμὸς
	703	τειρομένοις ἑτάροισιν ἀμυνέμεν,........
XXI	65	.... περὶ δ' ἤθελε θυμῷ
	66	ἐκφυγέειν θάνατόν τε κακὸν καὶ κῆρα μέλαιναν.
	177	...................τὸ δὲ τέταρτον ἤθελε θυμῷ
	178	ἄξαι ἐπιγνάμψας δόρυ μείλινον Αἰακίδαο,
XXIII	894	εἰ σύ γε σῷ θυμῷ ἐθέλοις·................
XXIV	236	......................περὶ δ' ἤθελε θυμῷ
	237	λύσασθαι φίλον υἱόν..................
xi	204	Ὣς ἔφατ'· αὐτὰρ ἐγὼ γ' ἔθελον φρεσὶ μερμήριξας
	205	μητρὸς ἐμῆς ψυχὴν ἐλέειν κατατεθνηυίης.
xiii	40	ἤδη γὰρ τετέλεσται ἅ μοι φίλος ἤθελε θυμός,
xiv	445	ὅττι κεν ᾧ θυμῷ ἐθέλῃ·................
xxi	273	οἱ δ' ἐπεὶ οὖν σπεῖσάν τ' ἔπιόν θ' ὅσον ἤθελε θυμός,
xxiv	511	ὄψεαι, αἴ κ' ἐθέλησθα, πάτερ φίλε, τῳδ' ἐνὶ θυμῷ
	512	οὔ τι καταισχύνοντα τεὸν γένος, ὡς ἀγορεύεις.
Theog.	446	........................θυμῷ γ' ἐθέλουσα,

πείθω

IV	104	Ὣς φάτ' Ἀθηναίη, τῷ δὲ φρένας ἄφρονι πείθειν·
VI	51	Ὣς φάτο, τῷ δ' ἄρα θυμὸν ἐνὶ στήθεσσιν ἔπειθε·
VII	120	Ὣς εἰπὼν παρέπεισεν ἀδελφειοῦ φρένας ἥρως
	121	αἴσιμα παρειπών, ὁ δ' ἐπείθετο·...........
IX	184	ῥηϊδίως πεπιθεῖν μεγάλας φρένας Αἰακίδαο.
	386	οὐδέ κεν ὣς ἔτι θυμὸν ἐμὸν πείσει' Ἀγαμέμνων,
	587	ἀλλ' οὐδ' ὣς τοῦ θυμὸν ἐνὶ στήθεσσιν ἔπειθον,
XII	173	Ὣς ἔφατ', οὐδὲ Διὸς πεῖθε φρένα ταῦτ' ἀγορεύων·
XIII	788	Ὣς εἰπὼν παρέπεισεν ἀδελφειοῦ φρένας ἥρως·
XVI	842	ὥς πού σε προσέφη, σοὶ δὲ φρένας ἄφρονι πεῖθε.
XXII	78	.... οὐδ' Ἕκτορι θυμὸν ἔπειθε.
	91	.... οὐδ' Ἕκτορι θυμὸν ἔπειθεν
vii	258	ἀλλ' ἐμὸν οὔ ποτε θυμὸν ἐνὶ στήθεσσιν ἔπειθεν.
ix	33	
	500	Ὣς φάσαν· ἀλλ' οὐ πεῖθον ἐμὸν μεγαλήτορα θυμόν,
xiv	290	ὅς μ' ἄγε παρπεπιθὼν ᾗσι φρεσίν,..........
xxiii	230	πείθεις δή μευ θυμόν, ἀπηνέα περ μάλῳ ἐόντα.
	337	ἀλλὰ τοῦ οὔ ποτε θυμὸν ἐνὶ στήθεσσιν ἔπειθεν·
H.Dem.	329	ἀλλ' οὔτις πεῖσαι δύνατο φρένας οὐδὲ νόημα
	330	θυμῷ χωομένης,........................

APPENDIX

ἀνέχω, τολμάω, τλάω, τλήμων, τλητός

XVIII	430	τοσσάδ' ἐνὶ <u>φρεσὶν</u> ᾗσιν <u>ἀνέσχετο</u> κήδεα λυγρά,
XXIV	518	ᾶ δείλ', ᾖ δὴ πολλὰ κάκ' <u>ἄνσχεο</u> σὸν κατὰ <u>θυμόν</u>,
X	232	......αἰεὶ γάρ οἱ ἐνὶ <u>φρεσὶ θυμὸς ἐτόλμα</u>.
XVII	68	ὡς τῶν οὔ τινι <u>θυμὸς</u> ἐνὶ στήθεσσιν <u>ἐτόλμα</u>
	69	ἀντίον ἐλθέμεναι Μενελάου κυδαλίμοιο.
xvii	284	<u>τολμήεις</u> μοι <u>θυμός</u>, ἐπεὶ κακὰ πολλὰ πέπονθα
	285	κύμασι καὶ πολέμῳ·......................
I	227	οὔτε λόχονδ' ἰέναι σὺν ἀριστήεσσιν Ἀχαιῶν
	228	<u>τέτληκας θυμῷ</u>·.........................
iv	447	πᾶσαν δ' ἠοίην μένομεν <u>τετληότι θυμῷ</u>.
	459	ἡμεῖς δ' ἀστεμφέως ἔχομεν <u>τετληότι θυμῷ</u>.
ix	434	.....αὐτὰρ χερσὶν ἀώτου θεσπεσίοιο
	435	νωλεμέως στρεφθεὶς ἐχόμην <u>τετληότι θυμῷ</u>
xi	181	καὶ λίην κείνη γε μένει <u>τετληότι θυμῷ</u>
	182	σοῖσιν ἐνὶ μεγάροισιν·...............
xviii	135	καὶ τὰ φέρει ἀεκαζόμενος <u>τετληότι θυμῷ</u>.
xix	347	ἥ τις δὴ <u>τέτληκε</u> τόσα <u>φρεσὶν</u> ὅσσα τ' ἐγὼ περ·
xxiii	100	οὐ μέν κ' ἄλλη γ' ὧδε γυνὴ <u>τετληότι θυμῷ</u>
	101	ἀνδρὸς ἀφεσταίη,........................
	168	
	169	
xxiv	162	αὐτὰρ ὁ τῆος <u>ἐτόλμα</u> ἐνὶ μεγάροισιν ἑοῖσι
	163	βαλλόμενος καὶ ἐνισσόμενος <u>τετληότι θυμῷ</u>·
V	669	...............νόησε δὲ δῖος Ὀδυσσεὺς
	670	<u>τλήμονα θυμὸν</u> ἔχων, μαίμησε δέ οἱ φίλον ἦτορ·
XXIV	49	<u>τλητὸν</u> γὰρ Μοῖραι <u>θυμὸν</u> θέσαν ἀνθρώποισιν.

χόλος, χολόω, χώομαι

I	216	χρὴ μὲν σφωίτερόν γε, θεά, ἔπος εἰρύσσασθαι
	217	καὶ μάλα περ <u>θυμῷ κεχολωμένον</u>·...........
IV	494	τοῦ δῴ Ὀδυσεὺς μάλα <u>θυμὸν</u> ἀποκταμένοιο <u>χολώθη</u>,
XIII	660	Τοῦ δὲ Πάρις μάλα <u>θυμὸν</u> ἀποκταμένοιο <u>χολώθη</u>·
XVI	60	............................οὐδ' ἄρα πως ἦν
	61	ἀσπερχὲς <u>κεχολῶσθαι</u> ἐνὶ <u>φρεσὶν</u>·..............
vi	147	μή οἱ γοῦνα λαβόντι <u>χολώσαιτο φρένα</u> κούρη.
ix	480	Ὣς ἐφάμην· ὁ δ' ἔπειτα <u>χολώσατο κηρόθι μᾶλλον</u>·
xvii	458	Ὣς ἔφατ'· Ἀντίνοος δ' <u>ἐχολώσατο κηρόθι</u> μᾶλλον,
xviii	387	Ὣς ἔφατ'· Εὐρύμαχος δ' <u>ἐχολώσατο κηρόθι</u> μᾶλλον,
xxii	224	Ὣς φάτ'· Ἀθηναίη δὲ <u>χολώσατο κηρόθι</u> μᾶλλον,
Erga	47	ἀλλὰ Ζεὺς ἔκρυψε, <u>χολωσάμενος φρεσὶν</u> ᾗσιν,
Theog.	568	...............<u>ἐχόλωσε</u> δέ μιν φίλον <u>ἦτορ</u>,
II	241	ἀλλὰ μάλ' οὐκ Ἀχιλῆϊ <u>χόλος φρεσὶν</u>, ἀλλὰ μεθήμων·
VI	326	δαιμόνι', οὐ μὲν καλὰ <u>χόλον</u> τόνδ' ἔνθεο <u>θυμῷ</u>.
IX	436	...............ἐπεὶ <u>χόλος</u> ἔμπεσε <u>θυμῷ</u>,
	675	.........<u>χόλος</u> δ' ἔτ' ἔχει μεγαλήτορα <u>θυμόν</u>;
XIV	49	.........ἦ ῥα καὶ ἄλλοι ἐϋκνήμιδες Ἀχαιοὶ
	50	ἐν <u>θυμῷ</u> βάλλονται ἐμοὶ <u>χόλον</u>,...........
	207	...............ἐπεὶ <u>χόλος</u> ἔμπεσε <u>θυμῷ</u>.
	306	
XVI	206	.....ἐπεί ῥά τοι ὧδε κακὸς <u>χόλος</u> ἔμπεσε <u>θυμῷ</u>.
xxiv	248	ἄλλο δέ τοι ἐρέω, σὺ δὲ μὴ <u>χόλον</u> ἔνθεο <u>θυμῷ</u>·
Theog.	554	<u>χώσατο</u> δὲ <u>φρένας</u> ἀμφί, <u>χόλος</u> δέ μιν ἵκετο <u>θυμόν</u>,
XVI	616	Αἰνείας δῴ ἄρα <u>θυμὸν ἐχώσατο</u> φώνησέν τε·
XX	29	νῦν δῴ ὅτε δὴ καὶ <u>θυμὸν</u> ἑταίρου <u>χώεται</u> αἰνῶς,
v	284	...............ὁ δῴ <u>ἐχώσατο κηρόθι</u> μᾶλλον,
Theog.	554	<u>χώσατο</u> δὲ <u>φρένας</u> ἀμφί, χόλος δέ μιν ἵκετο θυμόν,
H.Dem.	329	ἀλλῴ οὔτις πεῖσαι δύνατο <u>φρένας</u> οὐδὲ νόημα
	330	<u>θυμῷ χωομένης</u>:......................

πατάσσω, πτήσσω, δείδειν, τάρβω, τρομέω

VII	216	Ἕκτορί τ' αὐτῷ θυμὸς ἐνὶ στήθεσσι πάτασσεν·
XIII	282	ἐν δέ τέ οἱ κραδίη μεγάλα στέρνοισι πατάσσει
	283	κῆρας ὀϊομένῳ, πάταγος δέ τε γίγνετ' ὀδόντων·
XXIII	370	.... πάτασσε δὲ θυμὸς ἑκάστου
	371	νίκης ἱεμένων·............................
XIV	40	.... πτῆξε δὲ θυμὸν ἐνὶ στήθεσσιν Ἀχαιῶν.
I	555	νῦν δ' αἰνῶς δείδοικα κατὰ φρένα μή σε παρείπῃ
VIII	138	δεῖσε δ' ὅ γ' ἐν θυμῷ, Διομήδεα δὲ προσέειπε·
IX	244	ταῦτ' αἰνῶς δείδοικα κατὰ φρένα, μή οἱ ἀπειλὰς
X	538	ἀλλ' αἰνῶς δείδοικα κατὰ φρένα μή τι πάθωσιν
XIII	163	.... δεῖσε δὲ θυμῷ
	164	ἔγχος Μηριόναο δαΐφρονος·................
	623	.... οὐδέ τι θυμῷ
	624	Ζηνὸς ἐριβρεμέτεω χαλεπὴν ἐδείσατε μῆνιν
	625	ξεινίου,..................................
XV	298	.... τὸν δ' οἴω καὶ μεμαῶτα
	299	θυμῷ δείσεσθαι Δαναῶν καταδῦναι ὅμιλον.
XXIV	672	.... μή πως δείσει' ἐνὶ θυμῷ.
	778	ἄξετε νῦν, Τρῶες, ξύλα ἄστυδε, μηδέ τι θυμῷ
	779	δείσητ' Ἀργείων πυκινὸν λόχον·...........
iv	825	θάρσει, μηδέ τι πάγχυ μετὰ φρεσὶ δείδιθι λίην·
xvi	306	ἠμὲν ὅπου τις νῶϊ τίει καὶ δείδιε θυμῷ,
	331	.... ἵνα μὴ δείσασ' ἐνὶ θυμῷ
	332	ἰφθίμη βασίλεια τέρεν κατὰ δάκρυον εἴβοι.
xxiv	353	νῦν δ' αἰνῶς δείδοικα κατὰ φρένα μὴ τάχα πάντες
XXI	574	.... οὐδέ τι θυμῷ
	575	ταρβεῖ οὐδὲ φοβεῖται,...................
xviii	330	.... οὐδέ τι θυμῷ
	331	ταρβεῖς· ἦ ῥά σε οἶνος ἔχει φρένας, ἤ νύ τοι αἰεὶ
	332	τοιοῦτος νόος ἐστίν, ὃ καὶ μεταμώνια βάζεις.
	390	
	391	
	392	
X	9	ὡς πυκίν' ἐν στήθεσσιν ἀναστενάχιζ' Ἀγαμέμνων
	10	νειόθεν ἐκ κραδίης, τρομέοντο δέ οἱ φρένες ἐντός.
	491	τὰ φρονέων κατὰ θυμόν, ὅπως καλλίτριχες ἵπποι
	492	ῥεῖα διέλθοιεν μηδὲ τρομεοίατο θυμῷ
	493	νεκροῖς ἐμβαίνοντες·....................
XV	627	.... τρομέουσι δέ τε φρένα ναῦται
	628	δειδιότες·...............................
XXIV	152	μηδέ τί οἱ θάνατος μελέτω φρεσὶ μηδέ τι τάρβος·
	181	

ἀκαχέω

XII	179	.... θεοὶ δ' ἀκάχητο θυμὸν
XVIII	29	θυμὸν ἀκηχέμεναι μεγάλ' ἴαχον,............
xvi	342	Μνηστῆρες δ' ᾧ ἀκάχοντο κατήφησάν τῷ ἐνὶ θυμῷ,

ἀκαχίζομαι

VI	486	δαιμονίη, μή μοί τι λίην ἀκαχίζεο θυμῷ·
ix	62	Ἔνθεν δὲ προτέρω πλέομεν ἀκαχήμενοι ἦτορ
	105	
	565	
x	77	
	133	
	313	...... αὐτὰρ ἐγὼν ἑπόμην ἀκαχήμενος ἦτορ.
xiii	286	..... αὐτὰρ ἐγὼν λιπόμην ἀκαχήμενος ἦτορ.
xv	481	
xx	84	.... πυκινῶς ἀκαχήμενος ἦτορ,

APPENDIX

ἀχεύω
V	398	αὐτὰρ ὁ βῆ πρὸς δῶμα Διὸς καὶ μακρὸν Ὄλυμπον
	399	κῆρ ἀχέων, ὀδύνῃσι πεπαρμένος.............
	869	πὰρ δὲ Διὶ Κρονίωνι καθέζετο θυμὸν ἀχεύων,
XVIII	446	ἤτοι ὅ τῆς ἀχέων φρένας ἔφθιεν·...........
	461	.... ὁ δὲ κεῖται ἐπὶ χθονὶ θυμὸν ἀχεύων.
XXIII	566	τοῖσι δὲ καὶ Μενέλαος ἀνίστατο θυμὸν ἀχεύων,
	567	Ἀντιλόχῳ ἄμοτον κεχολωμένος·...........
xi	195	ἔνθ' ὅ γε κεῖτ' ἀχέων, μέγα δὲ φρεσὶ πένθος ἀέξει
xxi	318	μηδέ τις ὑμείων τοῦ γ' εἵνεκα θυμὸν ἀχεύων
Erga	399	μή ποτε σὺν παίδεσσι γυναικί τε θυμὸν ἀχεύων

ἄχνυμαι
I	102	ἥρως Ἀτρεΐδης εὐρὺ κρείων Ἀγαμέμνων
	103	ἀχνύμενος· μένεος δὲ μέγα φρένες ἀμφὶ μέλαιναι
	104	πίμπλαντ', ὄσσε δε οἱ πυρὶ λαμπετόωντι ἐΐκτην·
VI	523	.... τὸ δ' ἐμὸν κῆρ
	524	ἄχνυται ἐν θυμῷ,.....................
XIV	38	.........................ἄχνυτο δέ σφι
	39	θυμὸς ἐνὶ στήθεσσιν................
iv	660	τοῖσιν δ' Ἀντίνοος μετέφη Εὐπείθεος υἱός
	661	ἀχνύμενος - μένεος δὲ μέγα φρένες ἀμφιμέλαιναι
	662	πίμπλαντ', ὄσσε δε οἱ πυρὶ λαμπετόωντι ἐΐκτην-:
x	67	Ὣς φάσαν· αὐτὰρ ἐγὼ μετεφώνεον ἀχνύμενος κῆρ.
xii	153	δὴ τότ' ἐγὼν ἑτάροισι μετηύδων ἀχνύμενος κῆρ·
	270	
	250	.... τότε γ' ὕστατον, ἀχνύμενοι κῆρ.
xxii	188	.... ἐν δαπέδῳ δὲ χαμαὶ βάλον ἀχνύμενον κῆρ.
xxiv	420	αὐτοὶ δ' εἰς ἀγορὴν κίον ἀθρόοι, ἀχνύμενοι κῆρ.
Theog.	623	δηθὰ μάλ' ἀχνύμενοι, κραδίῃ μέγα πένθος ἔχοντες.

κήδω, ὀδύρομαι, ὀλοφύρομαι, στεναχίζομαι, συγχέω
V	399	.... αὐτὰρ ὀϊστὸς
	400	ὤμῳ ἔνι στιβαρῷ ἠλήλατο, κῆδε δὲ θυμόν.
XI	458	αἷμα δέ οἱ σπασθέντος ἀνέσσυτο, κῆδε δὲ θυμόν.
XXIV	549	..... μηδ' ἀλίαστον ὀδύρεο σὸν κατὰ θυμόν·
viii	577	εἰπὲ δ' ὅ τι κλαίεις καὶ ὀδύρεαι ἔνδοθι θυμῷ
xiii	379	ἡ δὲ σὸν αἰεὶ νόστον ὀδυρομένη κατὰ θυμὸν
xviii	203	..............ἵνα μήκετ' ὀδυρομένη κατὰ θυμὸν
VIII	201	.... οὐδέ νυ σοί περ
	202	ὀλλυμένων Δαναῶν ὀλοφύρεται ἐν φρεσὶ θυμός.
VII	95	.......................μέγα δε στεναχίζετο θυμῷ.
IX	612	μή μοι σύγχει θυμὸν ὀδυρόμενος καὶ ἀχεύων,
XIII	808	ἀλλ' οὐ σύγχει θυμὸν ἐνὶ στήθεσσιν Ἀχαιῶν.

ἄλγος
IX	321	.....................ἐπεὶ πάθον ἄλγεα θυμῷ,
XIII	670	....................ἵνα μὰ πάθοι ἄλγεα θυμῷ
XVI	55	.....................ἐπεὶ πάθον ἄλγεα θυμῷ
XVIII	224	.... ὄσσοντο γὰρ ἄλγεα θυμῷ.
	397	.... τότ' ἂν πάθον ἄλγεα θυμῷ,
XXII	53	ἄλγος ἐμῷ θυμῷ καὶ μητέρι,..................
XXIV	522	.... ἄλγεα δ' ἔμπης
	523	ἐν θυμῷ κατακεῖσθαι ἐάσομεν ἀχνύμενοί περ·
	568	τῶ νῦν μή μοι μᾶλλον ἐν ἄλγεσι θυμὸν ὀρίνῃς,
i	4	πολλὰ δ' ὅ γ' ἐν πόντῳ πάθεν ἄλγεα ὃν κατὰ θυμόν
v	83	δάκρυσι καὶ στοναχῇσι καὶ ἄλγεσι θυμὸν ἐρέχθων.
ix	75	κείμεθ' ὁμοῦ καμάτῳ τε καὶ ἄλγεσι θυμὸν ἔδοντες.
x	143	
xii	427	ἦλθε δ' ἐπὶ Νότος ὦκα, φέρων ἐμῷ ἄλγεα θυμῷ,

72 APPENDIX

xiii	90	ὃς πρὶν μὲν μάλα πολλὰ πάθ' <u>ἄλγεα</u> ὃν κατὰ <u>θυμὸν</u>
	263	.............τῆς εἵνεκ' ἐγὼ πάθον <u>ἄλγεα θυμῷ</u>,
xiv	310	αὐτὰρ ἐμοὶ Ζεὺς αὐτός, ἔχοντί περ <u>ἄλγεα θυμῷ</u>,
xv	486	Εὔμαι', ἦ μάλα δή μοι ἐνὶ φρεσὶ θυμὸν ὄρινας
	487	ταῦτα ἕκαστα λέγων, ὅσα δὴ πάθες <u>ἄλγεα θυμῷ</u>.
xvii	12	.............ἐμὲ δ' οὔ πως ἔστιν ἅπαντας
	13	ἀνθρώπους ἀνέχεσθαι, ἔχοντά περ <u>ἄλγεα θυμῷ</u>.
xix	471	τὴν δ' ἅμα χάρμα καὶ <u>ἄλγος</u> ἕλε <u>φρένα</u>, τὼ δέ οἱ ὄσσε
	472	δακρυόφι πλῆσθεν,........................
xxi	87	.... ἥ τε καὶ ἄλλως
	88	κεῖται ἐν <u>ἄλγεσι θυμός</u>, ἐπεὶ φίλον ὤλεσ' ἀκοίτην.

<u>ἀνίη, ἄχος, κῆδος, μελέδημα, ὀδύνη, πένθος</u>

Theog.	611	ζώει ἐνὶ στήθεσσιν ἔχων ἀλίαστον <u>ἀνίην</u>
	612	<u>θυμῷ</u> καὶ <u>κραδίῃ</u>,..................
II	171	.......ἐπεί μιν <u>ἄχος κραδίην</u> καὶ <u>θυμὸν</u> ἵκανεν·
III	412	...........ἔχω δ' <u>ἄχε'</u> ἄκριτα <u>θυμῷ</u>.
VIII	124	Ἕκτορα δ' αἰνὸν <u>ἄχος</u> πύκασε <u>φρένας</u> ἡνιόχοιο·
	316	
	147	ἀλλὰ τόδ' αἰνὸν <u>ἄχος κραδίην</u> καὶ <u>θυμὸν</u> ἱκάνει·
XIII	86	καὶ σφιν <u>ἄχος</u> κατὰ <u>θυμὸν</u> ἐγίγνετο..........
XIV	475	.... Τρῶας δ' <u>ἄχος</u> ἔλλαβε <u>θυμόν</u>.
XV	208	ἀλλὰ τόδ' αἰνὸν <u>ἄχος κραδίην</u> καὶ <u>θυμὸν</u> ἱκάνει,
XVI	52	
XVII	83	Ἕκτορα δ'αἰνὸν <u>ἄχος</u> πύκασε <u>φρένας</u> ἀμφὶ μελαίνας·
XIX	125	ὣς φάτο, τὸν δ' <u>ἄχος</u> ὀξὺ κατὰ <u>φρένα</u> τύψε βαθεῖαν·
XXIV	91	...................ἔχω δ' <u>ἄχε'</u> ἄκριτα <u>θυμῷ</u>.
xi	208	........ἐμοὶ δ' <u>ἄχος</u> ὀξὺ γενέσκετο <u>κηρόθι</u> μᾶλλον,
xviii	274	ἀλλὰ τόδ' αἰνὸν <u>ἄχος κραδίην</u> καὶ <u>θυμὸν</u> ἱκάνει·
	347	.... ὄφρ' ἔτι μᾶλλον,
	348	δύῃ <u>ἄχος κραδίην</u> Λαερτιάδεω Ὀδυσῆος.
xx	285	
	286	
H.Dem.	40	ὀξὺ δέ μιν <u>κραδίην ἄχος</u> ἔλλαβεν,...........
	90	τὴν δᾠ <u>ἄχος</u> αἰνότερον καὶ κύντερον ἵκετο <u>θυμόν</u>
	436	ἀμφαγαπαζόμεναι· <u>ἀχέων</u> δ' ἀπεπαύετο <u>θυμός</u>.
XVIII	8	μὴ δή μοι τελέωσι θεοὶ κακὰ <u>κήδεα θυμῷ</u>,
	430	τοσσάδ' ἐνὶ <u>φρεσὶν</u> ᾗσιν ἀνέσχετο <u>κήδεα</u> λυγρά,
viii	149	ἀλλ' ἄγε πείρησαι, σκέδασον δᾠἀπὸ <u>κήδεα θυμοῦ</u>·
ix	12	σοὶ δ' ἐμὰ <u>κήδεα θυμὸς</u> ἐπετράπετο στονόεντα
	13	εἴρεσθ', ὄφρ' ἔτι μᾶλλον ὀδυρόμενος στεναχίζω.
xiv	197	οὔ τι διαπρήξαιμι λέγων ἐμὰ <u>κήδεα θυμοῦ</u>,
XXIII	62	εὖτε τὸν ὕπνος ἔμαρπτε, λύων <u>μελεδήματα θυοῦ</u>,
iv	650	ὁππότ' ἀνὴρ τοιοῦτος ἔχων <u>μελεδήματα θυμῷ</u>,
xx	56	Εὖτε τὸν ὕπνος ἔμαρπτε, λύων <u>μελεδήματα θυμοῦ</u>,
xxiii	342	τοῦτ'ἄρα δεύτατον εἶπεν ἔπος, ὅτε οἱ γλυκὺς ὕπνος
	343	λυσιμελὴς ἐπόρουσε, λύων <u>μελεδήματα θυμῷ</u>.
ii	79	νῦν δέ μοι ἀπρήκτους <u>ὀδύνας</u> ἐμβάλλετε <u>θυμῷ</u>.
xix	117	μή μοι μᾶλλον <u>θυμὸν</u> ἐνιπλήσῃς <u>ὀδυνάων</u>
	118	μνησαμένῳ· μάλα δ' εἰμὶ πολύστονος·.........
I	362	τέκνον, τί κλαίεις; τί δέ σε <u>φρένας</u> ἵκετο <u>πένθος</u>;
XVIII	73	
	88	νῦν δ' ἵνα καὶ σοὶ <u>πένθος</u> ἐνὶ <u>φρεσὶ</u> μυρίον εἴη
	89	παιδὸς ἀποφθιμένοιο,.....................
XXII	242	ἀλλ' ἐμὸς ἔνδοθι <u>θυμὸς</u> ἐτείρετο <u>πένθει</u> λυγρῷ.
vii	218	καὶ μάλα τειρόμενον καὶ ἐνὶ <u>φρεσὶ πένθος</u> ἔχοντα·
	219	ὡς καὶ ἐγὼ <u>πένθος</u> μὲν ἔχω <u>φρεσίν</u>,...........
xi	195	ἔνθ' ὅ γε κεῖτ' ἀχέων, μέγα δὲ <u>φρεσὶ πένθος</u> ἀέξει
xvii	470	οὐ μὰν οὔτ' ἄχος ἐστὶ μετὰ <u>φρεσὶν</u> οὔτε τι <u>πένθος</u>,
xviii	324	ἀλλ' οὐδ' ὡς ἔχε <u>πένθος</u> ἐνὶ <u>φρεσὶ</u> Πηνελοπείης,

APPENDIX

xxiv	423	παιδὸς γάρ οἱ ἄλαστον ἐνὶ φρεσὶ πένθος ἔκειτο,
H.Aphr.	207	Τρῶα δὲ πένθος ἄλαστον ἔχε φρένας,........

II. Passages Containing Verbs of Inner Debate, Chapter III, Sections 67–72

ὁρμαίνω

X	507	ᾗος ὁ ταῦθ' ὥρμαινε κατὰ φρένα, τόφρα δ' Ἀθήνη
XI	411	
XVII	106	
XVIII	15	
XIV	20	ὡς ὁ γέρων ὥρμαινε δαϊζόμενος κατὰ θυμὸν
	21	διχθάδι', ἢ μεθ' ὅμιλον ἴοι Δαναῶν ταχυπώλων,
XVI	435	διχθὰ δέ μοι κραδίη μέμονε φρεσὶν ὁρμαίνοντι,
XXIV	680	ὁρμαίνοντ' ἀνὰ θυμὸν ὅπως Πρίαμον βασιλῆα
iii	151	νύκτα μὲν ἀέσαμεν χαλεπὰ φρεσὶν ὁρμαίνοντες
	152	ἀλλήλοις·................................
iv	120	*Ἠος ὁ ταῦθ' ὥρμαινε κατὰ φρένα καὶ κατὰ θυμόν,
v	365	*Ἠος ὁ ταῦθ' ὥρμαινε κατὰ φρένα καὶ κατὰ θυμόν,
	424	
iv	843	Τηλεμάχῳ φόνον αἰπὺν ἐνὶ φρεσὶν ὁρμαίνοντες.
v	365	*Ἠος ὁ ταῦθῳ ὥρμαινε κατὰ φρένα καὶ κατὰ θυμόν,
vi	118	ἑζόμενος δ' ὥρμαινε κατὰ φρένα καὶ κατὰ θυμόν·

μερμηρίζω

I	188	Ὡς φάτο· Πηλείωνι δ' ἄχος γένετ', ἐν δέ οἱ ἦτορ
	189	στήθεσσιν λασίοισι διάνδιχα μερμήριξεν,
II	3	ἀλλ' ὅ γε μερμήριζε κατὰ φρένα ὥς Ἀχιλῆα
	4	τιμήσῃ,.....................
V	671	μερμήριξε δ' ἔπειτα κατὰ φρένα καὶ κατὰ θυμόν.
VIII	169	τρὶς μὲν μερμήριξε κατὰ φρένα καὶ κατὰ θυμόν,
XIII	455	Ὡς φάτο, Δηίφοβος δὲ διάνδιχα μερμήριξεν
i	427	ἔνθ' ἔβη εἰς εὐνὴν πολλὰ φρεσὶ μερμηρίζων.
x	49	.....................αὐτὰρ ἐγώ γε
	50	ἐγρόμενος κατὰ θυμὸν ἀμύμονα μερμήριξα
	151	μερμήριξα δ' ἔπειτα κατὰ φρένα καὶ κατὰ θυμὸν
	152	ἐλθεῖν ἠδὲ πυθέσθαι,.....................
	438	Ὡς ἔφατ'· αὐτὰρ ἐγώ γε μετὰ φρεσὶ μερμήριξα
xi	204	Ὡς ἔφατ'· αὐτὰρ ἐγώ γ' ἔθελον φρεσὶ μερμηρίξας
xvi	73	μητρὶ δ' ἐμῇ δίχα θυμὸς ἐνὶ φρεσὶ μερμηρίζει,
	237	καί κεν ἐμὸν κατὰ θυμὸν ἀμύμονα μερμηρίξας
	238	φράσσομαι,........................
xx	10	πολλὰ δὲ μερμήριζε κατὰ φρένα καὶ κατὰ θυμόν,
	38	ἀλλά τί μοι τόδε θυμὸς ἐνὶ φρεσὶ μερμηρίζει,
	93	μερμήριζε δ' ἔπειτα , δόκησε δέ οἱ κατὰ θυμὸν
xxii	333	..................δίχα δὲ φρεσὶ μερμήριζεν,
xxiv	235	μερμήριζε δ' ἔπειτα κατὰ φρένα καὶ κατὰ θυμὸν
	236	κύσσαι καὶ περιφῦναι ἑὸν πατέρ',.............

III. Passages Containing Verbs of Motivation, Chapter III, Sections 73–81

ἀνώγω

IV	263	.........ὡς περ ἐμοί, πιέειν ὅτε θυμὸς ἀνώγοι.
VI	439	ἤ νυ καὶ αὐτῶν θυμὸς ἐποτρύνει καὶ ἀνώγει.
	444	οὐδέ με θυμὸς ἄνωγεν, ἐπεὶ μάθον ἔμμεναι ἐσθλὸς
VII	74	τῶν νῦν ὅν τινα θυμὸς ἐμοὶ μάχεσθαι ἀνώγει.
VIII	189	οἶνόν τ' ἐγκεράσασα πιεῖν, ὅτε θυμὸς ἀνώγοι,
	322	βῆ δ' ἰθὺς Τεύκρου, βαλέειν δέ ἑ θυμὸς ἀνώγει.
IX	101	κρῆναι δὲ καὶ ἄλλῳ, ὅτ' ἄν τινα θυμὸς ἀνώγῃ
	102	εἰπεῖν εἰς ἀγαθόν·...................
	702	.....τότε δ' αὖτε μαχήσεται, ὁππότε κέν μιν
	703	θυμὸς ἐνὶ στήθεσσιν ἀνώγῃ καὶ θεὸς ὄρσῃ.

APPENDIX

XIV	195	.... τελέσαι δέ με <u>θυμός</u> <u>ἀνώγεν</u>,
XV	43	ἀλλά που αὐτὸν <u>θυμός</u> ἐποτρύνει καὶ <u>ἀνώγει</u>,
XVIII	90	.... ἐπεὶ οὐδ' ἐμὲ <u>θυμός</u> ἄνωγε
	91	ζώειν οὐδ' ἄνδρεσσι μετέμμεναι, ...
	176	.... κεφαλὴν δέ ἑ <u>θυμός</u> ἄνωγε
	177	πῆξαι ἀνὰ σκολόπεσσι ταμόνθ' ἁπαλῆς ἀπὸ δειρῆς.
XIX	102	ὄφρ' εἴπω τά με <u>θυμός</u> ἐνὶ στήθεσσιν <u>ἀνώγει</u>.
XX	77	.... τοῦ γάρ ρα μάλιστά ἑ <u>θυμός</u> <u>ἀνώγει</u>
	78	αἵματος ἆσαι Ἄρηα ταλαύρινον πολεμιστήν.
	179	..... ἤ σέ γε <u>θυμός</u> ἐμοὶ μαχέσθαι <u>ἀνώγει</u>
XXII	142	....................ἐλέειν τέ ἑ <u>θυμός</u> <u>ἀνώγει</u>·
XXIV	140	εἰ δὴ πρόφρονι <u>θυμῷ</u> Ὀλύμπιος αὐτὸς <u>ἀνώγει</u>.
	198	αἰνῶς γάρ μ' αὐτὸν γε <u>μένος</u> καὶ <u>θυμός</u> ἄνωγε
i	316	δῶρον δ' ὅττι κέ μοι δοῦναι φίλον <u>ἦτορ</u> <u>ἀνώγῃ</u>,
v	89	αὔδα ὅ τι φρονέεις· τελέσαι δέ με <u>θυμός</u> ἄνωγεν,
viii	70	πὰρ δὲ δέπας οἴνοιο, πιεῖν ὅτε <u>θυμός</u> <u>ἀνώγοι</u>.
xi	206	τρὶς μὲν ἐφορμήθην, ἑλέειν τέ με <u>θυμός</u> <u>ἀνώγει</u>,
xiv	245	.... αὐτὰρ ἔπειτα
	246	Αἴγυπτόνδε με <u>θυμός</u> <u>ἀνώγει</u> ναυτίλλεσθαι,
xv	395	τῶν δ' ἄλλων ὅντινα <u>κραδίη</u> καὶ <u>θυμός</u> <u>ἀνώγει</u>,
xvi	141	...............ὅτε <u>θυμός</u> ἐνὶ στήθεσσιν <u>ἀνώγοι</u>·
	466	.... τάχιστά με <u>θυμός</u> <u>ἀνώγει</u>
	467	ἀγγελίην εἰπόντα πάλιν δεῦρ' ἀπονέεσθαι.
xviii	408	ἀλλ' εὖ δαισάμενοι κατακείετε οἴκαδ' ἰόντες,
	409	ὁππότε <u>θυμός</u> ἄνωγε·..................
xxi	194	...............φάσθαι δέ με <u>θυμός</u> <u>ἀνώγει</u>.
Theog.	549	τῶν δ' ἕλευ ὁπποτέρην σε ἐνὶ <u>φρεσὶ</u> <u>θυμός</u> <u>ἀνώγει</u>.

ὀτρύνω

V	470	Ὣς εἰπὼν <u>ὄτρυνε</u> <u>μένος</u> καὶ <u>θυμὸν</u> ἑκάστου.
VI	72	
XI	291	
XV	514	
	667	
XVI	210	
	275	Ὣς εἰπὼν <u>ὄτρυνε</u> <u>μένος</u>καὶ <u>θυμὸν</u> ἑκάστου,
XIII	155	Ὣς εἰπὼν <u>ὤτρυνε</u> <u>μένος</u> καὶ <u>θυμὸν</u> ἑκάστου.
XV	500	
V	792	ὣς εἰποῦσ' <u>ὄτρυνε</u> <u>μένος</u> καὶ <u>θυμὸν</u> ἑκάστου.
viii	15	
X	220	Νέστορ, ἔμ' <u>ὀτρύνει</u> <u>κραδίη</u> καὶ <u>θυμὸς</u> ἀγήνωρ
	319	Ἕκτορ, ἔμ' <u>ὀτρύνει</u> <u>κραδίη</u> καὶ <u>θυμὸς</u> ἀγήνωρ
XX	174	ὣς Ἀχιλῆ' ὄτρυνε <u>μένος</u> καὶ <u>θυμὸς</u> ἀγήνωρ
XXIV	288	.... ἐπεὶ ἄρ' σέ γε <u>θυμὸς</u>
	289	<u>ὀτρύνει</u> ἐπὶ νῆας, ἐμεῖο μέν οὐκ ἐθελούσης.
xviii	61	ξεῖν', εἴ σ' <u>ὀτρύνει</u> <u>κραδίη</u> καὶ <u>θυμὸς</u> ἀγήνωρ
	62	τοῦτον ἀλέξασθαι,......................

ἀνίημι

II	276	οὔ θήν μιν πάλιν αὖτις <u>ἀνήσει</u> <u>θυμὸς</u> ἀγήνωρ
VI	256	...............σὲ δ' ἐνθάδε <u>θυμὸς</u> <u>ἀνῆκεν</u>
VII	25	ἦλθες ἀπ' Οὐλύμποιο, μέγας δέ σε <u>θυμὸς</u> <u>ἀνῆκεν</u>;
	152	ἀλλ' ἐμὲ <u>θυμὸς</u> <u>ἀνῆκε</u> πολυτλήμων πολεμίζειν
X	389	.... ἦ σ' αὐτὸς <u>θυμὸς</u> <u>ἀνῆκε</u>;
XII	307	ὥς ρα τότ' ἀντίθεον Σαρπηδόνα <u>θυμὸς</u> <u>ἀνῆκε</u>
XV	24	.... ἐμὲ δ' οὐδ' ὣς <u>θυμὸν</u> <u>ἀνίει</u>
XVI	691	ὅς οἱ καὶ τότε <u>θυμὸν</u> ἐνὶ στήθεσσιν <u>ἀνῆκεν</u>.
XXI	395	...............μέγας δέ σε <u>θυμὸς</u> <u>ἀνῆκεν</u>;
XXII	252	...............νῦν αὖτέ με <u>θυμὸς</u> <u>ἀνῆκε</u>
	346	αἲ γάρ πως αὐτόν με <u>μένος</u> καὶ <u>θυμὸς</u> <u>ἀνείη</u>

APPENDIX   75

κελεύω, κέλομαι

VII	68	ὄφρ' εἴπω τά με θυμός ἐνὶ στήθεσσι κελεύει.
	349	
	369	
VIII	6	
vii	187	
viii	27	
xvii	469	
xviii	352	
xxi	276	
Theog.	645	
XIII	784	νῦν δ' ἄρχ', ὅππη σε κραδίη θυμός τε κελεύει·
viii	204	τῶν δ' ἄλλων ὅτινα κραδίη θυμός τε κελεύει,
xiv	517	πέμψει δ' ὅππη σε κραδίη θυμός τε κελεύει.
xv	339	
xvi	81	πέμψω δ' ὅππη σε κραδίη θυμός τε κελεύει.
xxi	342	
xxi	198	εἴπαθ' ὅπως ὑμέας κραδίη θυμός τε κελεύει.
X	534	ψεύσομαι, ἦ ἔτυμον ἐρέω; κέλεται δέ με θυμός.
iv	140	
XII	300	.... κέλεται δέ ἑ θυμὸς ἀγήνωρ
XIX	187	ταῦτα δ' ἐγὼν ἐθέλω ὀμόσαι, κέλεται δέ με θυμός,

ἐφρομάομαι

XIII	73	καὶ δ' ἐμοὶ αὐτῷ θυμὸς ἐνὶ στήθεσσι φίλοισι
	74	μᾶλλον ἐφορμᾶται πολεμίζειν ἠδὲ μάχεσθαι,
i	275	.... εἴ οἱ θυμὸς ἐφορμᾶται γαμέεσθαι,
iv	712	οὐ οἶδ' ἤ τίς μιν θεὸς ὤρορεν ἦε καὶ αὐτοῦ
	713	θυμὸς ἐφωρμήθη ἴμεν ἐς Πύλον, ...

ἐποτρύνω

VI	439	ἤ νυ καὶ αὐτῶν θυμὸς ἐποτρύνει καὶ ἀνώγει.
XV	43	ἀλλὰ που αὐτὸν θυμὸς ἐποτρύνει καὶ ἀνώγει,
i	88	αὐτὰρ ἐγὼν Ἰθάκην ἐσελεύσομαι, ὄφρα οἱ υἱὸν
	89	μᾶλλον ἐποτρύνω, καὶ οἱ μένος ἐν φρεσὶ θείω,
viii	44	............τῷ γάρ ῥα θεὸς πέρι δῶκεν ἀοιδὴν
	45	τέρπειν, ὅππη θυμὸς ἐποτρύνησιν ἀείδειν.
ix	138	ἀλλ' ἐπικέλσαντας μεῖναι χρόνον εἰς ὅ κε ναυτέων
	139	θυμὸς ἐποτρύνῃ καὶ ἐπιπνεύσωσιν ἀῆται.

ἐπισσεύω

I	173	φεῦγε μάλ', εἴ τοι θυμὸς ἐπέσσυται, ...
VI	361	ἤδη γάρ μοι θυμὸς ἐπέσσυται ὄφρ' ἐπαμύνω
IX	42	εἰ δέ τοι αὐτῷ θυμὸς ἐπέσσυται ὥς τε νέεσθαι,
	398	ἔνθα δέ μοι μάλα πολλὸν ἐπέσσυτο θυμὸς ἀγήνωρ

ὀρίνω

II	142	Ὣς φάτο, τοῖσι δὲ θυμὸν ἐνὶ στήθεσσιν ὄρινε
	143	πᾶσι μετὰ πληθύν, ...
III	395	Ὣς φάτο, τῇ δ' ἄρα θυμὸν ἐνὶ στήθεσσιν ὄρινε·
IV	208	
XI	804	Ὣς φάτο, τῷ δ' ἄρα θυμὸν ἐνὶ στήθεσσιν ὄρινε·
XIII	468	
V	28	.... τὸν δὲ κτάμενον παρ' ὄχεσφι,
	29	πᾶσιν ὀρίνθη θυμός· ....
IX	595	τοῦ δ' ὠρίνετο θυμὸς ἀκούοντος κακὰ ἔργα,
XI	792	τίς δ' οἶδ' εἴ κέν οἱ σὺν δαίμονι θυμὸν ὀρίναις
	793	παρειπών; ....
XIII	418	Ἀντιλόχῳ δὲ μάλιστα δαΐφρονι θυμὸν ὄρινεν·
XIV	459	Αἴαντι δὲ μάλιστα δαΐφρονι θυμὸν ὄρινε,

APPENDIX

	487	Πηνέλεῳ δὲ μάλιστα δαΐφρονι <u>θυμὸν</u> ὄρινεν·
XV	403	τίς δ' οἶδ' εἴ κέν οἱ σὺν δαίμονι <u>θυμὸν ὀρίνω</u>
	404	παρειπών;...............................
XVI	280	πᾶσιν <u>ὀρίνθη θυμός</u>, ἐκίνηθεν δὲ φάλαγγες,
	509	<u>ὠρίνθη</u> δέ οἱ <u>ἦτορ</u>,........................
XVII	123	'Ὣς ἔφατ', Αἴαντι δὲ δαΐφρονι <u>θυμὸν ὄρινε</u>·
XVIII	223	πᾶσιν <u>ὀρίνθη θυμός</u>·....................
XXIV	467	................ἵνα οἱ σὺν <u>θυμὸν ὀρίνῃς</u>.
	568	τῶ νῦν μή μοι μᾶλλον ἐν ἄλγεσι <u>θυμὸν ὀρίνῃς</u>,
	585	...............Ἀχιλῆΐ δ' <u>ὀρινθείη</u> φίλον <u>ἦτορ</u>,
iv	366	.... τῇ γάρ ῥα μάλιστά γε <u>θυμὸν ὄρινα</u>.
viii	178	<u>ὤρινάς</u> μοι <u>θυμὸν</u> ἐνὶ στήθεσσι φίλοισιν
	179	εἰπὼν οὐ κατὰ κόσμον................
xiv	361	ἂ δειλὲ ξείνων, ἦ μοι μάλα <u>θυμὸν ὄρινας</u>
	362	ταῦτα ἕκαστα λέγων,....................
xv	486	Εὔμαι', ἦ μάλα δή μοι ἐνὶ <u>φρεσὶ θυμὸν ὄρινας</u>
	487	ταῦτα ἕκαστα λέγων, ὅσα δὴ πάθες ἄλγεα θυμῷ.
xvii	46	μῆτερ ἐμή, μή μοι γόον <u>ὄρνυθι</u> μηδέ μοι <u>ἦτορ</u>
	47	ἐν στήθεσσιν <u>ὄρινε</u> φυγόντι περ αἰπὺν ὄλεθρον·
	150	Ὣς φάτο, τῇ δ' ἄρα <u>θυμὸν</u> ἐνὶ στήθεσσιν <u>ὄρινε</u>.
	216	......................<u>ὄρινε</u> δὲ κῆρ 'Οδυσῆος·
xviii	75	Ὣς ἄρ' ἔφαν· Ἴρῳ δὲ κακῶς <u>ὠρίνετο θυμός</u>.
xx	9	τοῦ δ' <u>ὠρίνετο θυμὸς</u> ἐνὶ στήθεσσι φίλοισι·
xxiv	318	τοῦ δ' <u>ὠρίνετο θυμός</u>,..................
H.Apol.	524	Τῶν δ' <u>ὠρίνετο θυμὸς</u> ἐνὶ στήθεσσι φίλοισι·

IV. Passages from Hesiod containing words connected with weather:

Ἔργα

	504	μῆνα δὲ Ληναιῶνα, κάκ' ἤματα, βουδόρα πάντα,
	505	τοῦτον ἀλεύασθαι, και πηγάδας, αἵ τ' ἐπὶ γαῖαν
	506	<u>πνεύσαντος</u> Βορέαο δυσηλεγέες τελέθουσιν,
	507	ὅς τε διὰ Θρήκης ἱπποτρόφου εὐρέϊ πόντῳ
	508	<u>ἐμπνεύσας ὤρινε</u>· μέμυκε δὲ γαῖα καὶ ὕλη·
	517	........................οὐ διάησιν
	518	ἲς <u>ἀνέμου</u> Βορέω·....................
	550	ὅς τε ἀρυσσάμενος ποταμῶν ἀπὸ αἰεναόντων,
	551	ὑψοῦ ὑπὲρ γαίης ἀρθεὶς <u>ἀνέμοιο θυέλλῃ</u>
	552	ἄλλοτε μέν θ' ὕει ποτὶ ἕσπερον, ἄλλοτ' <u>ἄησιν</u>
	553	πυκνὰ Θρηικίου Βορέω νέφεα κλονέοντος
	619	εὖτ' ἂν Πληιάδες σθένος ὄβριμον Ὠρίωνος
	620	φεύγουσαι πίπτωσιν ἐς ἠεροειδέα πόντον,
	621	δὴ τότε παντοίων <u>ἀνέμων θυίουσιν ἀῆται</u>·
	624	νῆα δ' ἐπ' ἠπείρου ἐρύσαι πυκάσαι τε λίθοισιν
	625	πάντοθεν, ὄφρ' ἴσχωσ' <u>ἀνέμων</u> μένος ὑγρὸν <u>ἀέντων</u>,
	626	χείμαρον ἐξερύσας, ἵνα μὴ πύθῃ Διὸς ὄμβρος·
	645	........εἴ κ' <u>ἄνεμοί</u> γε <u>κακὰς</u> ἀπέχωσιν <u>ἀήτας</u>.
	674	μηδὲ μένειν οἶνόν τε νέον καὶ ὀπωρινὸν ὄμβρον
	675	καὶ χειμῶν' ἐπίοντα Νότοιό τε δεινὰς <u>ἀήτας</u>,
	676	ὅς τ' <u>ὤρινε</u> θάλασσαν ὁμαρτήσας Διὸς ὄμβρῳ
	677	πολλῷ ὀπωρινῷ, χαλεπὸν δέ τε πόντον ἔθηκεν.

Θεογονία

	108	εἴπατε δ' ὡς τὰ πρῶτα θεοὶ καὶ γαῖα γένοντο
	109	καὶ ποταμοὶ καὶ πόντος ἀπείριτος οἴδματι <u>θυίων</u>
	110	ἄστρά τε λαμπετόωντα καὶ οὐρανὸς εὐρὺς ὕπερθεν·
	268	αἵ ῥ' <u>ἀνέμων πνοιῇσι</u> καὶ οἰωνοῖς ἅμ' ἕπονται
	269	ὠκείῃς πτερύγεσσι·....................
	319	ἡ δὲ Χίμαιραν ἔτικτε <u>πνέουσαν</u> ἀμαιμάκετον πῦρ,
	320	δεινήν τε μεγάλην τε ποδώκεά τε κρατερήν τε.
	323	[πρόσθε λέων, ὄπισθεν δὲ δράκων, μέσσῃ δὲ χίμαιρα,

324 δεινὸν ἀποπνείουσα πυρὸς μένος αἰθομένοιο.]
378 Ἀστραίῳ δ' Ἠὼς ἀνέμους τέκε καρτεροθύμους,

BIBLIOGRAPHY

TEXTS

Hesiod. 1967. *Fragmenta Hesiodea*, ed. R. Merkelbach and M. L. West, Oxford.
———. 1966. *Theogony*, ed. M. L. West, Oxford.
———. 1978. *Works and Days*, ed. M. L. West, Oxford.
Homer. 1962. *Opera*, v. 1, third ed., D. B. Munro and T. W. Allen, Oxford.
———. 1978. *Opera*, v. 2, third ed., D. B. Munro and T. W. Allen, Oxford.
———. 1961, *Opera*, v. 5, ed. T. W. Allen, Oxford.
———. *Odyssey*, vols. 1 and 2, ed. W. B. Stanford, 2nd ed., Edinburgh, 1974.
Pindar. 1971. *Epinicia cum Fragmentis*, 2 vols., ed. B. Snell and H. Maehler, Leipzig.

TRANSLATIONS

H. G. Evelyn-White. 1964. ed. and trans. of *Hesiod, the Homeric Hymns and Homerica*, London.
Fitzgerald, R. 1963. trans. of *The Odyssey* of Homer, Garden City, N. Y.
Lattimore, R. 1966. trans. of *The Iliad* of Homer, Chicago.
———. 1975, trans. of *The Odyssey* of Homer, New York.

REFERENCE WORKS

Chantraine, P. 1968. *Dictionnaire Etymologique de la Langue Grecque*, Paris.
Cunliffe, R. J. 1963. *A Lexicon of the Homeric Dialect*, Norman, Oklahoma.
Dunbar, H. 1971. ed. B. Marzullo. *A Complete Concordance to the Odyssey and the Hymns of Homer*, Hildesheim.
Liddell, Scott, and Jones. 1961. *A Greek-English Lexicon,* ninth ed., Oxford.
Minton, W. W. 1976. *Concordance to the Hesiodic Corpus*, Leiden.
Prendergast, G. L. 1983. ed. B. Marzullo. *A Complete Concordance to the Iliad of Homer*, Hildesheim.
Tebben, J. R. 1977. *A Computer Concordance to the Homeric Hymns*, Hildesheim.

BOOKS AND ARTICLES

Böhme, J. 1929. *Die Seele und das Ich im homeriscehn Epos mit einem Anhang: Vergleich mit dem Glauben der Primitiven*, Leipzig.
Bremmer, J. 1983. *The Early Greek Concept of the Soul*, Princeton.
Darcus, S. M. 1977. "Thumos and Psyche in Heraclitus B 85," *Rivista di Studi Classici* 25, 353–359.
———. 1977. "*Noos* Precedes *Phren* in Greek Lyric Poetry," *L'Antiquité Classique* 46 (1977), 41–51.
———. 1978. "The Phren of the Noos in Xenophanes' God," *Symbolae Osloenses* 53, 25–39.
———. 1978. "What Death Brings in Heraclitus," *Gymnasium* 85, 501–510.
———. 1978. "Heraclitus the Riddler," *Antike und Abendland* 24, 40–42.
———. 1979. "A Person's Relation to ψυχή in Homer, Hesiod, and the Greek Lyric Poets," *Glotta* 57, 30–39.Hesiod,
———. 1979. "A Person's Relation to φρήν in Homer, Hesiod and the Greek Lyric Poets," *Glotta* 57, 159–173.
———. 1979. "Logos of Psyche in Heraclitus," *Rivista Storica dell' Antichita* 9.1–2 (1979), 89–93.
———. 1980. "How a Person Relates to νόος in Homer, Hesiod, and the Greek Lyric Poets," *Glotta* 58, 33–46.
Detienne, M. and J.–P. Vernant. 1974. *Cunning Intelligence in Greek Culture and Society*, trans. Janet Lloyd, 1978, Sussex.
Frame, D. 1978. *The Myth of Return in Early Greek Epic*, New Haven.
Francis, E.D. 1983. "Virtue, Folly, and Greek Etymology," *Approaches to Homer*, ed. C. A. Rubino and C. W. Shelmerdine, Austin, 74–121.
Garland, R. 1981. "The Causation of Death in the *Iliad*: A Theological and Biological Investigation," *Bulletin of the Institute of Classical Studies* 28, University of London, 43–60.
Harrison, E. L. 1960. "Notes on Homeric Psychology," *The Phoenix*, 14.2, 63–80.

BIBLIOGRAPHY

Ireland, S., and Steel, F. L. D. 1975. "*Phrenes* as an Anatomical Organ in the Works of Homer," *Glotta* 53, 183–195.
Koch, H. J. 1976. "αἰπὺς ὄλεθρος and the Etymology of ὄλλυμι," *Glotta* 54, 216–222.
Nagler, M. N. 1974. *Spontaneity and Tradition*, Berkeley.
Nagy, G. 1970. *Greek Dialects and the Transformation of an Indo-European Process*, Cambrdige, Mass.
———. 1974. *Comparative Studies in Greek and Indic Meter*, Cambrdige, Mass.
———. 1979. *The Best of the Achaeans: Concepts of the Hero in Ancient Greek Poetry*, Baltimore.
———. 1980. "Patroklos, Concepts of Afterlife, and the Indic Triple Fire," *Arethusa* 13.2, 161–195.
———. 1981. "Another Look at *Kleos Aphthiton*," *Würzburger Jahrbücher für die Altertumswissenschaft*, n.f., 7, 113–116.
———. 1982. "Theognis of Megara: The Poet as Seer, Pilot, and Revenant," *Arethusa* 15,1 and 2, 109–128.
———. 1983. "On the Death of Sarpedon," *Approaches to Homer*, ed. C. A. Rubino and C. W. Shelmerdine, Austin, 189–217.
———. 1983. Sema and Noesis: Some Illustrations," *Arethusa* 16, 35–55.
Onians, R. B. 1954. *The Origins of European Thought*, Cambridge.
Renehan, R. 1979. "The Meaning of ΣΩΜΑ in Homer: A Study in Methodology," *California Studies in Classical Antiquity*, 12, 269–282.
Rix, H. "Hom. ὀρώρεται und die Verben ὄρνυμι und ὀρίνω, *Indogermanische Forschungen* 70.1 (1965), 25–49.
Rohde, E. 1920. *Psyche: The Cult of Souls and Belief in Immortality among the Greeks*, translated from the eighth edition by W. B. Hillis, New York, 1972.
Schnaufer, A. 1970. *Frühgriechischer Totenglaube: Untersuchungen zum Totenglauben der mykenischen und homerischen Zeit*, Hildesheim and New York.
Snell, B. 1953. *The Discovery of the Mind*, tr. T. G. Rosenmeyer, New York.
Solmsen, F. 1979. "Symphytos Aion (A., *Ag*. 106)," *American Journal of Philology* 100, 477–479.
Sourvinou-Inwood, C. 1972. Review of A. Schnaufer, *Frühgriechischer Totenglaube*, *Journal of Hellenic Studies* 92, 220–222.
Vermeule, Emily. 1979. *Aspects of Death in Early Greek Art and Poetry*, Berkeley.
Vernant, J.-P. 1981. *Mythe et Pensée chez les Grecs*, Paris.
Warden, J. 1971. "ΨΥΧΗ in Homeric Death Descriptions," *Phoenix* 25.2, 95–103.
Whitman, C. 1958. *Homer and the Homeric Tradition*, Cambridge, Mass.

INDEX

Anger, 31–32, 39–40. *See also* Rage
  stormy winds and, 52–53
Animals, death of, 15
Anima, 61, 62
Animus, 61, 62
Arbman, Ernst., 6

Battle, movement in, 59–60
Best of the Achaeans, The, 56
Bewitching, 32–33
Bickel, E., 5
Bile, 32
Blame, 41
Body-soul, 5, 8
Böhme, Joachim, 1, 2, 5–6, 11, 16
Boldness, 53
Breathing, 7, 14, 15–16, 22
Breeze, Latin term for, 61
Bremmer, Jan, 8

"Causation of Death in the *Iliad*, The: A Theological and Biological Investigation", 8, 11–12
Chantraine, Pierre, 12n, 13n, 19–20, 21n, 32
Cheyns, André, 8
Cognition, 11, 21–34, 50, 51–52, 61–62
  emotion and, 33–34
  impairment of, 35, 36, 50, 61
  terms for, 34
Conflict, 45. *See also* Inner debate
Consciousness, 8
Containment, 3, 43, 50, 52, 61–62
Criticism, 41

Darcus, Shirley, 8
Dead, soul of, 8
Death, 2–3, 8, 11, 12–16, 21, 49–50. *See also* Loss of Consciousness
  φρήν/φρένες and, 17–18
  storm winds and, 58
Deliberation, 3, 11, 29
Density of texture, 19
Devising, 30–31
Die Seele und das Ich im Homerischen Epos, 1, 5
Discovery of the Mind, The, 6

Eagerness, 37
Early Greek Concept of the Soul, The, 8
Emotion, 3, 11, 34–41, 50, 62
  cognition and, 33–34
  restraint of, 42–44
  violent, 63
Endurance, 39

Energy, 8
Eroticism, power of, 43–44
Exultation, 41

Flying, 15
Food and drink, 16–17
Frame, Douglas, 8
Free-soul, 8
Frühgriechischer Totenglaube: Untersuchungen zum Totenglaube der mykenischen und homerischen Zeit, 7
Fumus, 7, 51, 61

Garland, Robert, 8, 11–12, 15
Grief, 40–41, 44

Hades, 12, 14, 15, 19
Harrison, E. L., 25n
Heart, 18
Hesiod, 2, 39
Hinduism, 7
Homer, 1, 2, 4
Homeric Hymns, 2
Hunger, 35
Hymn to Demeter, 36, 39

Iliad, 2, 12, 13, 19, 22n, 26, 27, 34, 37, 38n, 39, 46–48, 51, 57, 58, 59
Inner debate, 44–47, 49, 50, 62
Inner wind, 4, 63. *See also* Wind
Intellect, 11, 22, 50. *See also* Cognition
  emotion and, 33
  impairment of, 61
Ireland, S., 8, 16n

Koch, H. J., 13n

Life-soul, 5–6, 61, 62
Longing, 35
Loss of consciousness, 2–3, 8, 11, 12, 15–16, 49–50. *See also* Death
  recovery from, 28

Mental activity, 19. *See also* Cognition
Motivation, 3, 11, 22–23, 47–49, 50, 53, 54, 62
Myth of Return in Early Greek Epic, The, 8

Nagy, Gregory, 8, 12n, 54n, 56
Nature and Culture in the Iliad, 1

Odyssey, 2, 21, 26, 36, 37, 38n, 39, 46, 47, 48, 52, 57

Onians, R. B., 1, 7, 11, 16
Origins of European Thought, The, 1, 7
Otto, W. F. 5

Pallor, 43
Passion, 35
"Patroklos," 8
Perception, 25, 33
Physiology, 16–21
Plan, 29–30
Plato, 51, 56
Pleasure, sensation of, 36–37
Praṇa, 7
Prayer, 41
Psyche, 5

Rage, 41. *See also* Anger
  storm winds and, 55
Recognition, 27, 28
Redfield, James M., 1
Renehan, Robert, 6
Restraint, 42–43
Revival, 14
Rohde, Erwin, 5, 6

Satiety, 38
Schnaufer, Albrecht, 7–8, 13n
Sea, storms at, 54, 56, 57, 58, 60
Self-mutilation, 41
Sexual desire, 35–36
Snell, Bruno, 6
Solmsen, F., 12n
Soul, 61, 62
  of dead vs. living, 8
South Wind, 56
Spencer, Herbert, 5
Steel, F. L. D., 8, 16n
Storm winds, 3, 48–51
  anger and, 52–53
  rage and, 55
  at sea, 56–58, 60
Subjugation, 43–44
Syncope, 12, 21

Threatening, 41
Trembling, 43

Underworld, 16, 50
Upanishads, 7

Vernant, Jean-Paul, 21n–22n

Weather, 48, 53. *See also* Storm winds; Winds
Winds, 3, 48–49, 50, 51–63. *See also* Storm winds
  blasts of, 54–55, 57
  characteristics shared with θυμός, 60
  inner, 4, 63
  Latin term for, 61
  scattering by, 58–59

θυμός as human counterpart of, 62–63
Wishing, 37

Yielding, 43–44

ἀασάμην, 31
ἀάζομαι, 32
ἀάζω, 22, 31, 60
ἄελλαι, 54
ἀεσίφρων, 31, 60
ἄημι, 52, 53, 54, 60, 61
ἀῆται, 54
ἄητο, 54
ἄητον, 54
ἄητον θάρσος, 54
ἄητος, 52
αἰδώς, 42
αἰεί, 12 n
αἴων, 12
αἰπὺς ὄλεθρος, 13n
ἀκαχίζω, 40
ἄλγος, 40
ἀλκή. 18
ἄλληκτος, 23, 31, 43, 52, 56, 60
ἀλύσσω, 41
ἀμφί, 18
ἀμφικαλύπτω, 18
ἄμπνυτο, 13n, 22
ἀμύσσω
ἀνα-, 13 n., 41
ἀνδάνω, 37
ἄνεμος, 61
ἀνέχω, 39
ἀνίημι, 48, 53, 54
ἀνώγω, 48
ἀπειλέω, 41
ἀπὸ τῆς θύσεως καὶ ζέσεως τῆς ψυχῆς, 11
(ἀπο)πέτομαι, 15
ἀραρίσκω, 19n
ἄτη, 19, 60
ἄφθιτα, 30n
ἀχεύω, 40
ἄχνυμαι, 40
ἄχος, 19, 40

βάλλομαι, 19n
βίη, 37
βλεμεαίνω, 41
βουλή 19, 29–30
βούλομαι, 37

γηθέω 28, 37
γηθοσύνη, 37
γηθόσυνος, 37
γιγνώσκω, 3, 22, 27–28

δαϊζόμενος, 45–46
δάκνω 40, 41
δαμάζω 3, 43–44

δια-, 47
διαλέγομαι, 45, 47
διάνδιχα, 45
διαρραίω, 58
δίχα, 45
διχθά, 45
διχθάδια, 46
δοκέω, 46

ἐθέλω 38
εἴδωλον, 14
ἐκ θυμοῦ φίλεον, 35
ἐκ θυμοῦ φιλέων, 35
ἔλπομαι, 38
ἔμπεδοι, 18, 19
ἔμπεδος, 21
ἐμπνύνθη, 13 n
ἔμπνυτο, 13 n
ἐνὶ φρεσί, 34, 48, 50
ἐνὶ στήθεσσι, 48, 50
ἐνθυμεῖσθαι, 25n
ἐνθύμημα, 25n
ἐνίπη 41
ἐπιπνείουσα, 54
ἐπισσεύω, 3, 48
ἐπισσεύομαι, 49, 53, 59, 60
ἔπος, 19
ἐποτρύνω, 3, 48, 53
ἐρέχθω, 52, 58, 60
ἐρητύω, 42–43
ἔρως, 18, 35–36
ἐς φρένα θυμὸς ἀγέρθη, 22
ἐσμαίομαι, 41
ἔτι γὰρ θεόθεν καταπνείει/πειθὼ μολπᾶν
    ἀλκᾶν σύμφυτος αἰών, 12
ἐφορμάομαι, 48
ἐφορμάω, 3

ἦτορ, 8, 17, 20
    deliberation and, 3
    death and, 5, 12
    food and drink and, 17
    physiology and, 20
    emotion and, 3, 34, 37, 39, 44, 50
    grief and, 41
    inner debate and, 46, 50
    motivation and, 47, 48, 49, 50

θάρσος, 54
θέλγω, 22, 32–33
θύελλα, 62, 63
θυμοδακὴς γὰρ μῦθος, 40
θυμοραϊστής, 52, 58, 60
θυμός
    bewitched, 32–33
    cognition and, 21–34, 50, 52, 61–62
    containment of, 3, 43, 50, 52, 61–62
    death and, 2–3, 8, 12–16, 21, 49–50

death of animals and, 15
deliberation and, 3, 11, 29
emotion and, 3, 33–34, 34–41, 50,
    51–52, 62
as energy, 8
failure to function, 51–52
food and drink and, 16–17
fumus and, 7, 51, 61
grief and, 40–41, 44
inner debate and, 45–47, 50, 62
as inner wind, 4, 63
intellect and, 50
loss of consciousness and, 2–3, 8, 11, 12,
    15–16, 49–50
manner of departure of, 15
motivation and, 3, 11, 22–23, 45–47, 50,
    53, 54, 62
as organ of ego, 6
physiology of, 16–21, 44
prana and, 7
previous studies of, 5–9
vs. ψυχή, 15–16, 22
relationship of φρήν/φρένες to, 3, 4, 7,
    43, 51–52, 60, 61
restraint of emotion and, 42–43
revival of, 14, 21
scattered by winds, 58–59
syncope, 12, 21
variety of definitions for, 1–4, 11–12, 63
weather and, 3, 48, 53
winds and storms and, 3, 51–63
θυμὸς ἐνὶ φρεσί, 24, 42–43, 46
θυμῷ νοέω, 26
θύω, 24, 39–40, 51, 52, 56, 57, 58, 62–63
θωρήσσω, 19n

ἰαίνω, 36–37
ἵεμαι, 37
ἵμερος, 35

κακός, 23, 43
καπνός, 54 n
καπύειν, 54 n
καπύω 12n
κατὰ φρένα καὶ κατὰ θυμόν, 26, 27, 45, 46
κατέδω, 40, 41
κῆδος, 40
κήδω, 40
κεκαδών, 13n
κεκαφηότα, 54
κεκαφηότα θυμόν, 12
κέλεται δέ ἑ θυμὸς ἀγήνωρ, 48
κέλεται δέ με θυμός, 48
κελεύω, 48
κέλομαι, 3, 48
κῆρ, 5, 8
    emotion and, 34, 37, 44, 50
    grief and, 41
    motivation and, 48, 49, 50
κηρόθι, 39

κοτεσσαμένη τό γε θυμῷ, 39
κραδίη, 5, 8
    cognition and, 22
    emotion and, 3, 33, 34, 36–37, 42–43, 44, 50
    grief and, 41
    inner debate and, 45, 47
    motivation and, 47, 48, 49, 50
    perception and, 25, 33
κραδίη θυμός τε κελέυει, 48

λανθάνω, 31
λευγαλέαι φρένες, 20
λευγαλέοι, 19–20
λευγαλέος, 20, 32
*λεῦγος, 20

μαίνομαι, 39
μανθάνω, 22
μεγαλίζομαι, 41
μέγα φρονέων, 55
μέλαιναι, 18
μελεδήμα, 40
μένος
    body-soul and, 8
    loss of consciousness/death and, 2–3, 12–13, 14, 16, 49
    motivation and, 3, 47, 50
    physiology and, 18
μένος ἠύ, 8
μερμηρίζειν, 38n
μέρμεριζω, 29, 45, 46, 47
μερμηρίξας, 38
μετὰ φρεσί, 34
μήδεα, 19, 30–31
μήδομαι, 30–31
μῆτις, 29
μῦθος πεπνυμένος, 52, 54

νεμεσάω, 41
νεμεσίζομαι, 41
νέομαι, 8
νοέω, 3, 22, 25, 26–27, 31
νόημα, 22, 23
νόος
    body-soul and, 8
    cognition and, 3, 22, 25, 26, 31, 34, 50, 61
    emotion and, 33, 37, 38, 39
    physiology and, 19
    sexual desire and, 36
    θυμός and, 27
νόστος, 25

ὀδύνη, 40
ὀδύρομαι, 40
οἶδα, 3, 22, 25, 26, 27
οἶδα κατὰ θυμόν, 24
ὄλλυμι, 13n
ὀλοιῇσι φρεσὶ θύει, 39
ὀλοφύρομαι, 40
ὀρίνω 3, 48–49, 52, 53, 55, 60

ὀρινομένη, 54
ὁρμαίνω, 45, 45–46, 47
ὀτρύνω, 3, 47–48, 49
οὐδέ με θυμός ἄνωγεν, 22–23
οὐκ νοέω, 31

πείθω, 38
πένθος, 40
πεπνυμένα, 26, 30
πεπνυμένος, 30, 61
πέπνυσαι νόῳ, 26
πνοιή, 53, 54
ποιέω, 19n
πόνος, 18
Ποντάρχης, 56
πόντος, 53, 55
πράπιδες, 7n
πύκα, 19
πυκιναί, 18, 19
πυκινός, 18–19, 19, 20

σεβάζομαι, 42
σέβας, 42
σῆμα ἰδών, 28
σθένος, 18
σιδήρεος, 23, 31, 43
στεναχίζω, 40
στήθεα, 22, 39
στῆθος, 22y
στρεπτός, 20
συνέχω, 40

τέρπομαι, 38
τέρπω, 37–38
τετληότι θυμῷ, 39
τί σφῶν ἐνὶ φρεσὶ μαίνεται ἦτορ, 39
τιτύσκομαι, 37
τλάω, 39
τλήμων, 39
τλητός, 39
τολμάω, 39

ὑφαίνω, 19

φθίω, 40
φιλέω, 3, 39–40
φράζω, 3, 22, 28–29
φράζομαι, 28
φράσσω, 46
φρεσί, 56
φρήν/φρένες, 5
    adjectives describing, 19, 22
    cognition and, 23–29, 31, 34, 50, 52, 61–62
    consciousness and, 50
    containment and, 3–4, 7, 43
    death and, 13, 17–18, 59
    deliberation and, 3
    emotion and, 34, 36–37, 38, 39, 40, 43, 44, 50, 62

INDEX

grief and, 41
heart and, 18
hunger in, 35
inner debate and, 46, 47, 50
λευγαλέαι, 20
as lungs, 7, 8
motivation and, 3, 47, 50
as organ of ego, 6
physical impairment of, 32, 52
physiology and, 16, 17
plan and, 29–30
revival and, 14
relationship of θυμός to, 3–4, 7, 43, 51–52, 60, 61
restraint of emotion and, 42–43
sexual desire and, 35–36
φρονέω, 3, 19, 22, 24, 28, 34

χάζομαι, 13n
χαίρω, 34, 37
χόλος, 39
χολόω, 39
χώομαι, 39

ψυχή, 51
   interpretation of, 5–6
   loss of consciousness/death and, 2, 8, 12–15, 49, 54n, 61, 62–63
   manner of departure of, 15
   vs. θυμός, 15–16, 22
ψύχω, 6, 51, 62

ὣς εἰπὼν ὄτρυνε μένος καὶ θυμὸν ἑκάστου, 47

		DATE DUE		

883.01
CAS
Supplements to Mnemosyne
Caswell, Caroline P.